ULTIMATE DINOSAURS
DIPLODOCUS

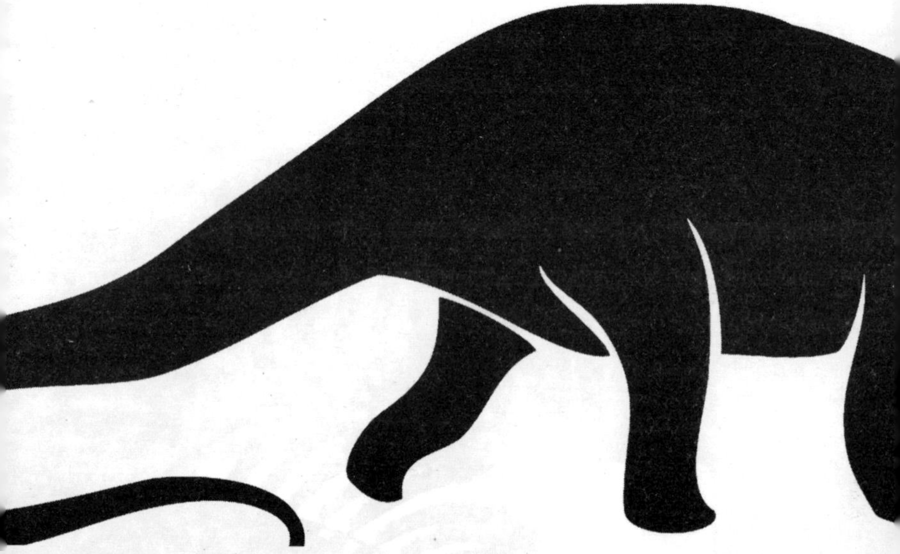

BEN GARROD

ULTIMATE DINOSAURS
DIPLODOCUS

ZEPHYR
An imprint of Head of Zeus

First published in the UK in 2018 by Zephyr, an imprint of Head of Zeus
This revised and updated Zephyr paperback edition first published in the UK
in 2023 by Head of Zeus, part of Bloomsbury Publishing Plc

Text © Ben Garrod, 2023

Palaeo Art © Scott Hartman, 2023, and Gabriel Ugueto, 2023

Cartoon illustrations © Ethan Kocak, 2023

The moral right of Ben Garrod to be identified as the author and
of Scott Hartman, Gabriel Ugueto and Ethan Kocak to be identified
as the artists of this work have been asserted in accordance with
the Copyright, Designs and Patents Act of 1988.

All rights reserved. No part of this publication may be
reproduced, stored in a retrieval system, or transmitted in any form
or by any means, electronic, mechanical, photocopying, recording,
or otherwise, without the prior permission of both the copyright
owner and the above publisher of this book.

9 8 7 6 5 4 3 2 1

A CIP catalogue record for this book is available from the British Library.

ISBN (PB): 9781804549667
ISBN (E): 9781035902682

Designed by Nicky Borowiec

Printed and bound in Great Britain
by CPI Group (UK) Ltd, Croydon CR0 4YY

MIX
Paper | Supporting
responsible forestry
FSC® C171272

Head of Zeus
5-8 Hardwick Street
London EC1R 4RG

WWW.HEADOFZEUS.COM

For the animals in our homes,
teaching us so much about nature

1 DINOSAUR DEFINITIONS   15

What *is* a Dinosaur?

Definitely Dinosaurs

Dino Checklist

2 DINOSAUR DETECTIVES   29

Diplodocus

Family Tree

Diplodocus Relatives

3 DINOSAUR DISCOVERIES   43

When and Where

ASK AN EXPERT: COULD A *BRONTOSAURUS* SIT ON YOUR LAP?   50

CONTENTS

4 DELVE INTO A DINOSAUR 55
Anatomy of *Diplodocus*

The Skeleton

The Body

5 DINOSAUR DOMAINS 75
Habitats and Ecosystems

NEW SCIENCE: NEW GIANT DINOSAUR DISCOVERIES 83

6 DODGING DINOSAURS 89
Evolutionary Arms Race

The Battle

FOSSIL FINDER 99
Quiz Answers **104**

Glossary **107**

Prof 'Boneboy' Ben is a very special geek indeed. Not a week goes by when I don't get on the phone to ask Prof Ben a question about obscure, strange aspects of biology, and he always has the answers. The reader of this book is very lucky to have such a terrific teacher!

The study of science makes sense of everything in our world. Science makes everything work, and the genius scientists behind technology genuinely are the most powerful people in the world . . .

INTRODUCTION
by STEVE BACKSHALL

Palaeontology, or dino-science, is not just about unearthing old stone bones, it's about understanding our planet, and everything that has ever lived on it. By bringing it to life for a new generation, Prof Ben is connecting you to our past, and making you a part of the knowledge of our future. As he says, there is nothing wrong with being clever; you should embrace your inner geek, and see the world as a puzzle waiting to be solved . . .

Enjoy the adventure.

HEY EVERYONE!

You know when you love something and can't remember when you first started liking it? Well, it's like that with me and science. Now I'm a scientist and I study animals and do TV programmes, but actually I can still remember the very first time I started to 'like' science.

I was about three years old and staying with my grandparents. My granddad, George, used to take me for walks on the beach, looking for shells and other things from the sea. I remember we'd just got home, it was raining and there were lots of little red worms on the garden path. I asked where they came from, because I'd never seen them when it wasn't raining. He said they were from the moon (now I realise this wasn't true) and I remember wondering how they got there, where

11

they went when there was no rain and what they ate, with mouths so small.

My point is that **you can love science** even **when you're really young** and even if you don't know much about what you're looking at (like me and the 'moon worms'). **Science is cool** because we can ask question after question after question and **the more we discover, the more we have still to ask**. So, if you're reading this and you love dinosaurs, it might be your first step to becoming a palaeontologist (a scientist who studies dinosaurs), a doctor, an astronaut (check for moon worms for me) or even a shark biologist.

That moon worms day was the first step for me in becoming a scientist. For you, it might be **finding a fossil** on a walk, seeing your pet do something weird or **watching a meteor shower** and that's it, you're hooked. Then, keep it up. **Keep reading about science or collecting things** or going out and exploring because believe me, it gets better and better.

You're never too young to begin.

I started a creepy-crawly zoo when I was about five. I had spiders, centipedes, pill bugs and even a very grumpy devil's coach horse, all in separate jars. I fed them, drew them in my notebook and released them safely, but for me, it was like capturing tigers, wolves and cobras. When I was about ten, my teacher brought in owl pellets and we looked at the bones inside to see what the birds had been eating. If you love science and do 'sciencey' things for fun, then you, my friend, are a scientist – it doesn't matter whether you're nine or ninety.

Now I'm an actual scientist and it's great. I have a job that's cool and makes me happy. I've lived in Africa, working with wild chimpanzees, studied coral reefs in Madagascar, and followed walruses up on Svalbard in the Arctic. I've helped save Sumatran orangutans in Indonesia and lived in the Caribbean, studying monkeys. I've watched teams dig up giant dinosaur bones in Argentina and I've seen scientists drill into the asteroid core that led to the end of the dinosaurs. **Every day, I wake up and look forward to new adventures**.

I still have as many questions about science as I did when I was growing up. My series *Ultimate Dinosaurs* looks at all the best-known dinosaur species as well as random weird ones and uses some of the most modern and interesting science to reveal how your favourite dinosaurs ate enough food every day to fill a skip, how they hunted in the dark and why some predators turned vegetarian. Amazing discoveries will show us what dinosaurs looked like, what colour they were and even what sounds they made. You are young scientists, so I've included the most up-to-date research and used some complicated terms. We'll tackle some difficult ideas, because I reckon you guys can handle it.

So, let's take a look at what life was like in the time of the dinosaurs.

Let's get geeky!

Ben

CHAPTER 1

DINOSAUR DEFINITIONS

WHAT *IS* A DINOSAUR?

Dinosaur Definitions

Imagine a conversation between you and your teacher. Maybe he knows a lot about dinosaurs but maybe not as much as you.

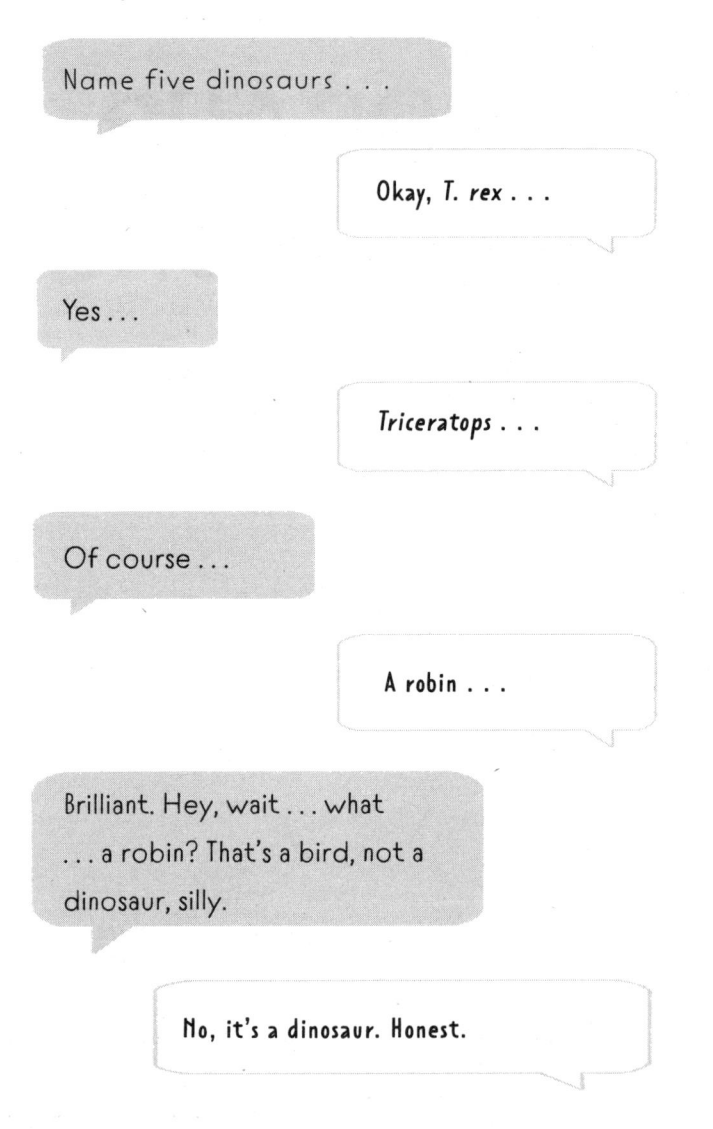

> Name five dinosaurs . . .

> Okay, *T. rex* . . .

> Yes . . .

> *Triceratops* . . .

> Of course . . .

> A robin . . .

> Brilliant. Hey, wait . . . what . . . a robin? That's a bird, not a dinosaur, silly.

> No, it's a dinosaur. Honest.

What *is* a Dinosaur?

> It can't be, I had one on my bird-feeder in my garden this morning.

> Cool. Still a dinosaur though.

> But they're cute – there was one on my Christmas card and everything.

> Erm . . .

> Robins can't be dinosaurs, they're birds.

> Yes, all dinosaurs. Robins, owls, gulls, hummingbirds, eagles . . . all dinosaurs.

> I need to lie down . . .

> You need to learn the new definition of a dinosaur, sir.

Dinosaur Definitions

Most of you will already know that birds are dinosaurs. They're not 'like' dinosaurs, they're not 'sort of' dinosaurs, they are living dinosaurs. You might even have had a similar conversation, where someone didn't believe you. In fact, try it now – ask an adult if birds are dinosaurs and see what their answer is. Let's have a quick look at how and why we can safely say that not all the dinosaurs died out 66 million years ago and that next time a gull steals your sandwich or you have a cute little bird at your window, you've actually just had a close encounter with a living dinosaur.

First, we have to get the term right – we consider birds to be 'avian dinosaurs' and that the ones that died out when the asteroid struck were 'non-avian dinosaurs'. So, technically, dinosaurs did and didn't die out 66 million years ago. This 'birds are dinosaurs' idea might seem random and recent but it's not a new idea. It's been around since the 19th century (even longer than your

What *is* a Dinosaur?

> If you look out of your window, there's a good chance you'll see a bird. There are about 10,000 species alive today but we think they may have originally evolved from dinosaurs like the dromaeosaurs. Obviously, they look very different now but over 150 million years, lots of changes happen.

parents), and Charles Darwin wrote about how similar birds looked to the 'classic' dinosaurs. As ever with science, things were argued and debated for years and it's only now that we have enough evidence to be pretty sure.

Not long after Darwin wrote his amazing book *The Origin of Species*, the first fossil of an *Archaeopteryx* was found in Germany. It had bones that looked like those of a bird and the fossil preserved the imprints of feathers, which also looked similar to those of a bird. Scientists went from identifying it as a close relative of birds, to saying it was the first of the birds . . . like the great, great, great (imagine saying 'great' for over a week) grandmother of all birds we see today. We know this second bit isn't true – it was an early bird, but it wasn't the first, because

Dinosaur Definitions

we have older fossils from earlier bird ancestors, after the avian dinosaurs split from the rest of the dinosaurs; things like *Aurornis* and *Anchiornis*.

If we want to look at the similarities between dinosaurs and early birds, then it's probably easiest to look at the

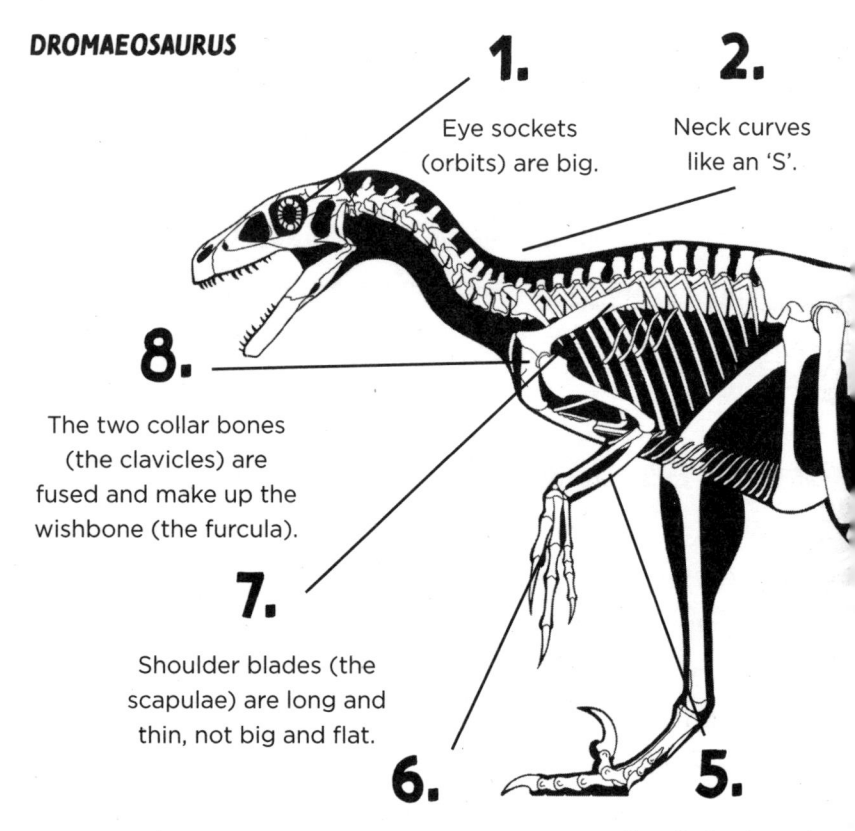

DROMAEOSAURUS

1. Eye sockets (orbits) are big.

2. Neck curves like an 'S'.

8. The two collar bones (the clavicles) are fused and make up the wishbone (the furcula).

7. Shoulder blades (the scapulae) are long and thin, not big and flat.

6. Hands have three fingers.

5. Forelimbs (arms) are long and have clawed 'hands'.

What *is* a Dinosaur?

bones – sometimes feathers are preserved but bones are the best fossil evidence we have. Here are some of the things scientists have seen in both early birds (such as the *Archaeopteryx*) and their closest dinosaur relatives (like *Dromaeosaurus*):

3.

A bone called the pubis (it's in the middle and on the bottom of the pelvis) is facing the back, rather than forwards, as in other animals. It looks as though it has a little boot on the end.

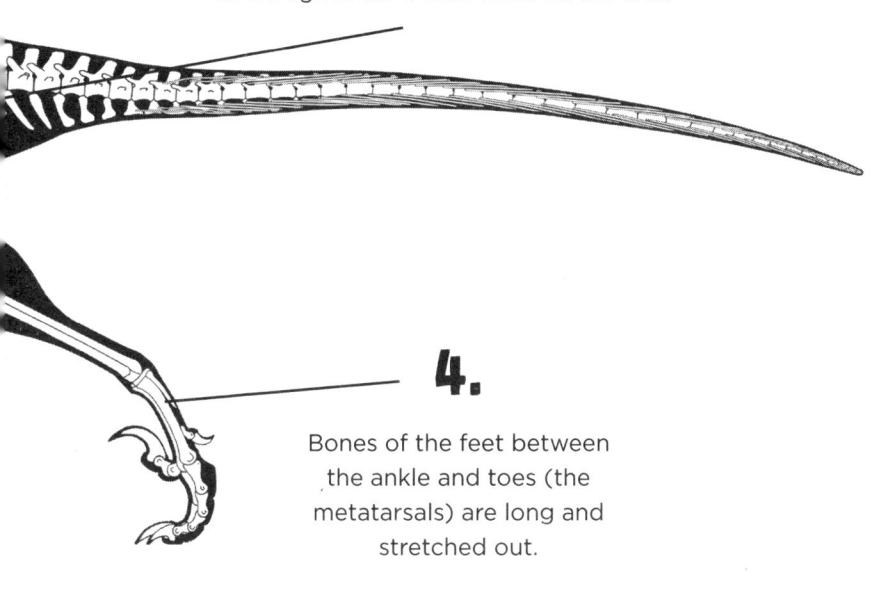

4.

Bones of the feet between the ankle and toes (the metatarsals) are long and stretched out.

Dinosaur Definitions

Very early members of the bird family and their closest non-avian dinosaur relatives had thin-walled bones that looked as though they were hollow. As well as the

> It's hard to understand how birds and non-avian dinosaurs are the same thing. How can a pigeon evolve from something like a *Velociraptor*? Well, it's like playing 'Chinese Whispers' . . . the more time that passes, the bigger the differences from where you started.
>
> You might start by saying something like 'Sailing is bad when it's foggy' but the last person thinks they hear 'On Sunday, my dad smells like a doggy'. The same happens in nature. Over millions of years, small changes are made every time a new generation is born (or hatches) and the thing at the end (like a flamingo) might look very different from the original (like a maniraptor). Start a chain of whispers and see what's happened by the end – it's a good way to think about how evolution works. Maybe try 'Flamingos evolved from things like a *T. rex* and both are dinosaurs'.

similarities in skeletons, both had similar hearts, brains, muscles, scales and laid eggs. Under a microscope, the shells of their eggs would look very similar.

The major differences are that most birds can fly and are endothermic (warm-blooded). There are other differences obviously, but what I'm trying to say is that birds and non-avian dinosaurs are really, really closely related.

> We know a lot about dinosaurs from their fossilised bones. But bones don't always last long enough to fossilise. They are made up from hard minerals and softer biological ingredients, such as collagen. To show this, drop a bone (maybe from a meal before it's cooked) into vinegar for at least 24 hours. All the minerals dissolve and only the collagen is left. Now, the bone will be squashy and bendable.

DEFINITELY DINOSAURS

So, birds are dinosaurs, hey? How do we know a *Diplodocus*, *T. rex*, *Oviraptor* and *Thecodontosaurus* are all dinosaurs but that a pterosaur isn't? Are pliosaurs dinosaurs or marine reptiles, and why is a chicken a dinosaur and not a mammal? We need to look at what makes a dinosaur a dinosaur.

There are lots of arguments over dinosaur definitions, because there were so many different species – some small enough to sit on your hand, some big enough to sit on your house (and smash it). Some could glide, some could swim, some could run. Many ate meat, but others ate plants. With so many different dinosaurs, it's hard to make an clear definition.

Try it for yourself – what's the difference between fruit and vegetables? Easy, right? But what about tomatoes? Exactly! Not so easy.

Scientists look at lots of things to see whether they have found a dinosaur fossil. Some seem really important and others look as though they couldn't possibly be important – but if we can tick them all off, then we can be 100 per cent sure it's a dinosaur.

DINO CHECKLIST

Some of these things are obvious on some fossils and almost impossible to see on others. To spot them, you will have to *really* know what to look for. Have a good look at a dinosaur fossil the next time you're at your local museum and then look at a crocodile or alligator skeleton and maybe a bird. Can you tick these things off in all these skeletons?

Dino diapsids. If you had x-ray vision and could look at your own skull in the mirror, you would see that you have a hole in your skull behind each eye. This means that we (like all mammals) are **synapsids**. But dinosaurs are **diapsids**. They have two holes behind each eye, towards the back of the skull. **(A)**

Between the two holes behind the eye, there is a dimple (called a **fossa**) in the bone. **(B)**

There is a ridge along the edge of the **humerus** (the upper arm bone) for big muscles to attach to. In dinosaurs, this ridge is more than 30 per cent along the bone. **(C)**

Dinosaur Definitions

(H)

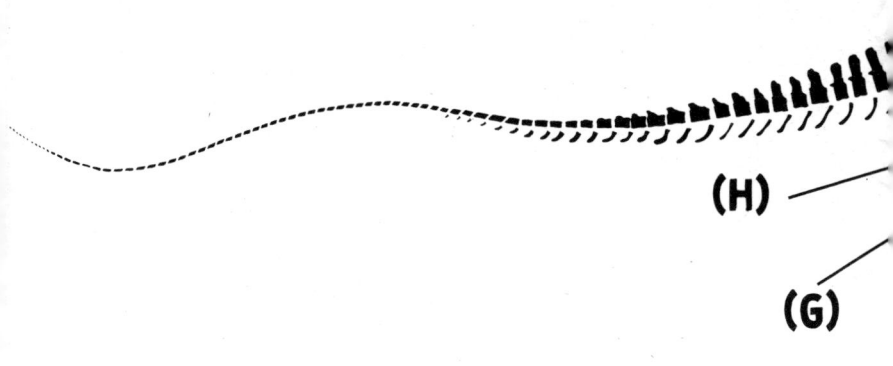

(G)

Teeny tiny arms. Almost every dinosaur had **forelimbs** (arms) slightly shorter than you might expect. For most dinosaurs, the **radius** bone (in the lower arm) is nearly always 20 per cent shorter than the **humerus** bone (in the upper arm). **(D)**

The ridge on the **tibia** (shin bone) curves to the front and outwards. **(E)**

At the place where the **fibula** (one of the lower leg bones) joins the ankle, there's a little dip on the ankle bone. **(F)**

Dino Checklist

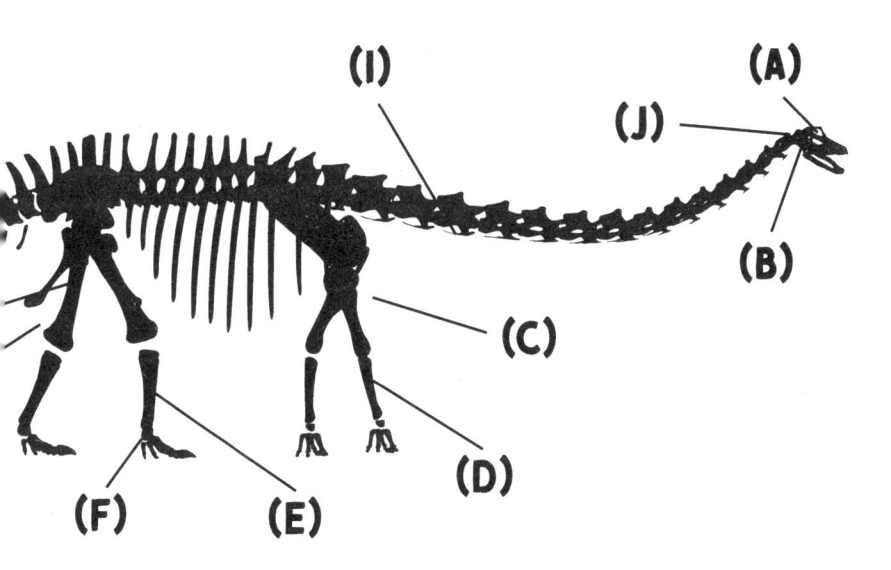

🐾 **Straight legs**. Have a look at people around you – their legs come straight down from their body, not out to the side like a crab. Dinosaurs were the same – their legs were straight, not out to the side. All reptiles (well, those with legs) have legs out to the side. **(G)**

🐾 The ridge (called the **fourth trochanter**) on the **femur** (thigh bone), which the big leg muscles attach to, is big and looks sharp. **(H)**

🐾 Most of the neck bones (**vertebrae**) have extra bits of bone that look like a diagonally backwards-facing wing on each side. These

27

Dinosaur Definitions

bits of bones are called '**epipophyses**' (*eppi-pofe ee-sees*). **(I)**

The bones at the back of the skull do not meet in the middle. **(J)**

That's how you define a dinosaur!

CHAPTER 2
DINOSAUR DETECTIVES

Diplodocus

If you ask people to name three or four different dinosaurs, most will include *Diplodocus* on their list. It's one of the best-known species of dinosaur. When we think of dinosaurs, it's usually either a two-legged carnivore like *T. rex* or a huge four-legged dinosaur with a long neck, long tail and a fat body, like a *Diplodocus*. Shout 'DINOSAUR' . . . and ask anyone nearby which dinosaur they immediately thought of.

The name *Diplodocus* is a bit of an odd one. It's a Latin word, made up from two Greek words, 'diplo-' (meaning '*double*') and '-dokus' (meaning '*beam*'). So, where is this *double beam*? And what is it? It refers to little bones called chevrons and there are lots of them on the underside of the tail. They look as though they have two coat-hangers strapped to them – these are the beams – and it is these that helped early palaeontologists identify *Diplodocus* as a separate species. Scientists first thought these special bones were only found in *Diplodocus*, but they have now seen them in other species too.

The first *Diplodocus* was discovered by Samuel Williston, in 1877. He was a palaeontologist (who also studied flies) and as well as discovering *Diplodocus*, he found the first *Allosaurus*. Imagine being the person to find both dinosaurs.

People often think that scientists are always right, but sometimes we get things wrong. And we got something wrong about *Diplodocus* from the start. The full scientific name of the first one found was *Diplodocus longus*, but now we only recognise two species – *Diplodocus carnegii* and *Diplodocus hallorum*. *Diplodocus longus* doesn't actually exist. Only a few small pieces of vertebrae from the tail of this first one were found, not enough to tell us very much. It was like guessing a mystery song from just three words. There definitely wasn't enough skeleton to understand much about the complete animal.

Dinosaur Detectives

Diplodocus hallorum
Diplodocus carnegii

Although *Diplodocus* wasn't the biggest of the sauropods, they were still pretty heavy (*Diplodocus carnegii* weighed 10–16 tonnes) and they were some of the longest dinosaurs. *Diplodocus carnegii* measured about 25m long (which is about the same length as a blue whale) but *Diplodocus hallorum* was even longer and could be as much as 32m (about the same as four double-decker buses end to end).

One of the most important parts of any skeleton is the skull. It can tell us so much about the species and the individual. We can look at how the animal could see, smell and hear and also what its diet was like. The only problem is that we don't have any *Diplodocus* skulls yet. Lots of other parts of the skeleton have been found and *Diplodocus* fossils are quite common but not the skull. Like all skulls, it's made up from lots of smaller bones and when the animal dies, either the head falls away from the body and is lost or it gets damaged easily. Maybe one day someone will be lucky enough to find the first skull of a *Diplodocus*.

FAMILY TREE

If you think about the two species of *Diplodocus*, they didn't just appear overnight. Every species evolves over time and slowly becomes different from all the others, and the *Diplodocus* is the same. That means that there are lots of other closely related dinosaurs in the *Diplodocus* family tree. The sauropods (which means '*lizard foot*') first appeared in the Late Triassic period and by the Late Jurassic, about 150 million years ago, the whole group was doing well, especially *Brachiosaurus* and its relatives and *Diplodocus* dinosaurs and their close relatives.

The sauropods are among the few groups of dinosaurs whose fossils can be found on every continent, including Antarctica. They survived up until the point when the famous asteroid struck Earth 66 million years ago. Towards the second half of their time on Earth, the more famous sauropods like *Brachiosaurus*, *Brontosaurus* and *Diplodocus* were extinct and the titanosaurs (the really big sauropods) were on the scene.

Dinosaur Detectives

It's easy to think that the sauropods were not as exciting as the theropods with their big claws and even bigger teeth, or the *Triceratops* and other horned dinosaurs that looked like angry armoured tanks on legs.

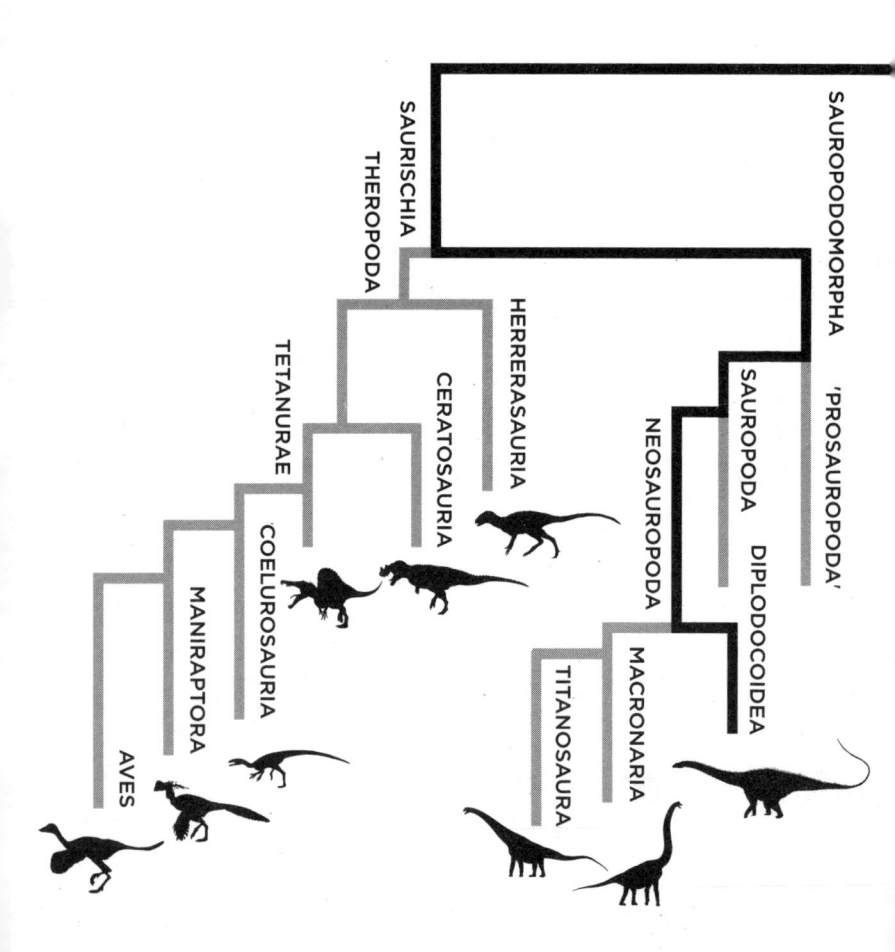

Family Tree

Sauropods were just like big prehistoric cows, weren't they – eating leaves all day and walking around not doing much? Well, no, not really. A look at *Diplodocus* shows us that sauropods were highly social animals

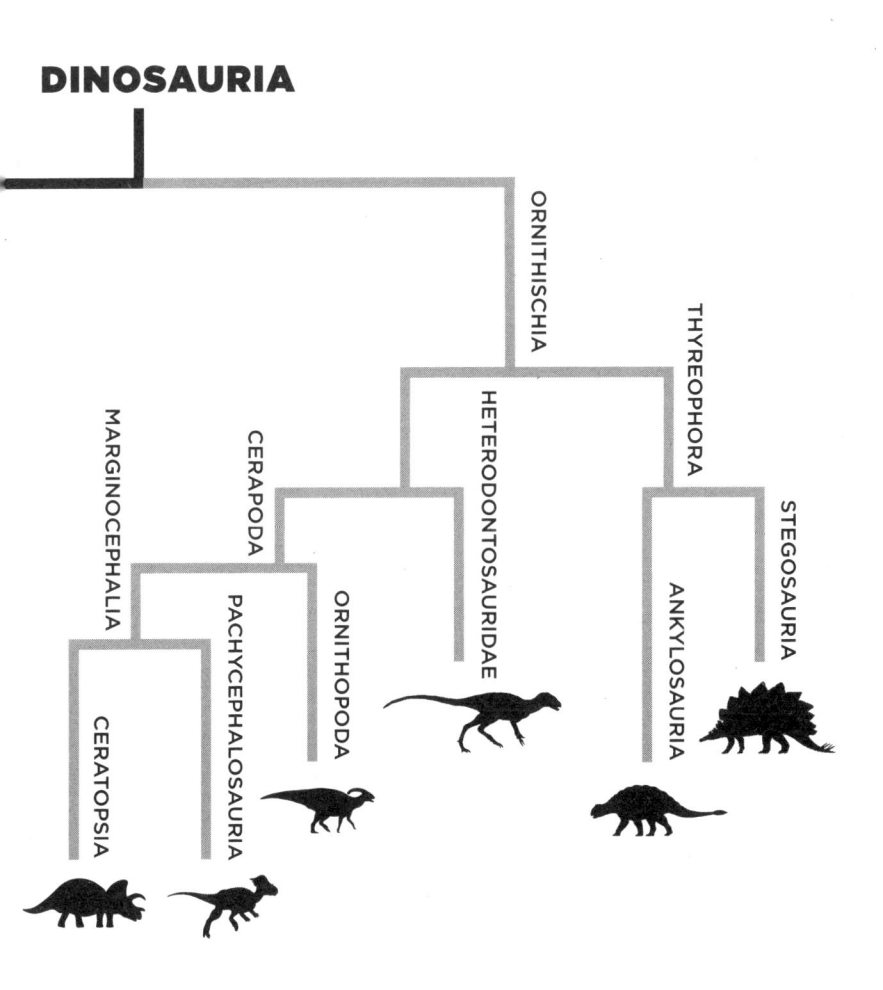

DINOSAURIA

DIPLODOCINAE

which lived in groups and had some very interesting anatomy that allowed them to become the biggest things ever to walk the planet. Some of these giant eating-machines were covered in spines, spikes and plates of armour made from bone. The sauropods are one of the most fascinating groups of dinosaurs and for me, *Diplodocus* is one of the coolest dinosaurs out there.

Not counting birds, there are about 1,000 species of dinosaurs that we know about so far. There are about 10,000 species of birds alive today, so there are probably loads more dinosaurs still to find out there. There's an argument about how we arrange all the dinosaur species (this is called 'taxonomy') but mainly, we agree there are two major groups – the *Ornithischia* (bird-hipped) and the *Saurischia* (lizard-hipped).

When you look at the family tree, the first weird thing that pops out is that we think the sauropods are more closely related to the two-legged theropods like *T. rex* (and birds) than they are to the dinosaur groups that

Family Tree

?????? (We know something was here but we haven't found fossils to prove it yet...)

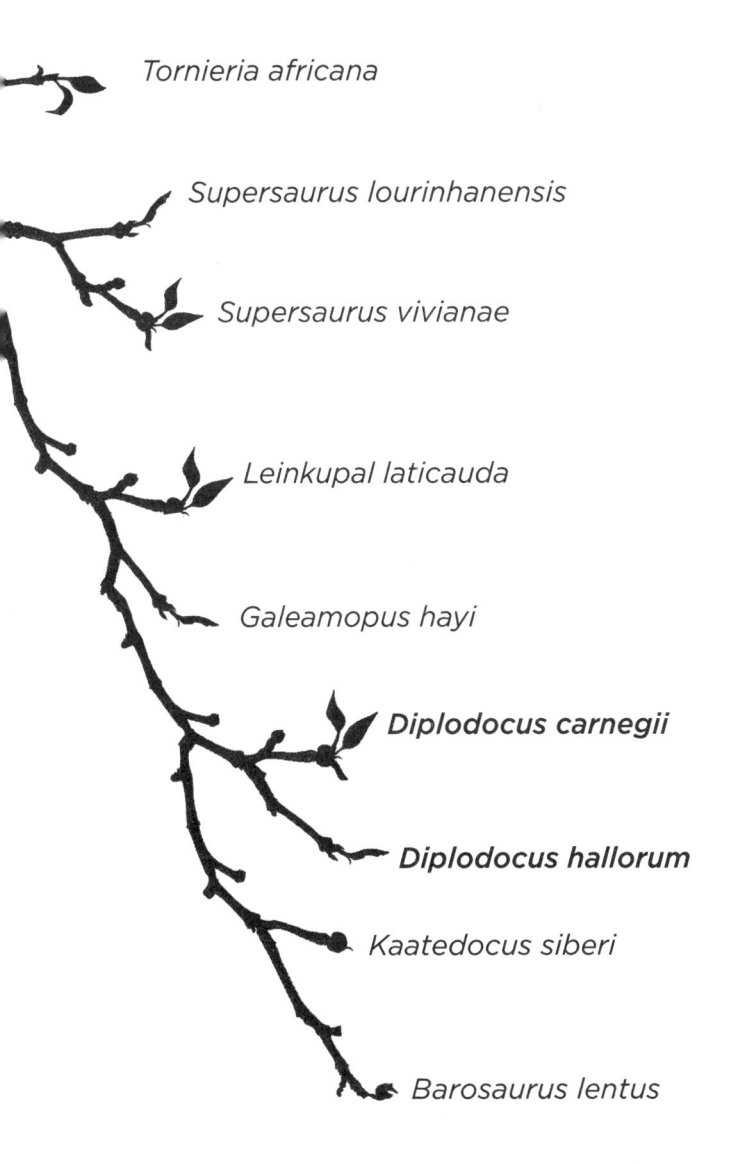

Tornieria africana

Supersaurus lourinhanensis

Supersaurus vivianae

Leinkupal laticauda

Galeamopus hayi

Diplodocus carnegii

Diplodocus hallorum

Kaatedocus siberi

Barosaurus lentus

include species such as *Stegosaurus* and *Triceratops*. Again, this might all change soon but we'll look at that in another book.

The branch of the dinosaur family tree that includes the sauropods also includes a branch with the prosauropods (which later evolved into the sauropods) and the giant sauropods, the titanosaurs.

The little branch at the end of the sauropod part of the dinosaur family tree finishes with a group called the Diplodocinae. There are nine (maybe ten) different species and all have the same basic shape – stretched-out, long sauropods, not tall like *Brachiosaurus* or giant like the titanosaurs. We talk about *Diplodocus* as if it is a single species but as you have already seen, there were two different species – *Diplodocus carnegii* and *Diplodocus hallorum*.

Diplodocus carnegii (*dip-low doke-us car-nee-gee*)
This was the better known of the two species of *Diplodocus* and was one of the longest dinosaurs to

have existed, reaching up to 25m in length. It was a medium-sized sauropod, 10–16 tonnes in weight.

In 1899, an almost complete skeleton was uncovered in the United States. Copies of this specimen have been made and are in museums all around the world now, in places like the Carnegie Museum of Natural History in the USA, the London Natural History Museum, the Natural Science Museum in Madrid, Spain and Senckenberg Museum in Frankfurt, Germany, for example. Many of these skeleton casts are called 'Dippy'.

Diplodocus hallorum (*dip-low doke-us hal-or-um*)
This diplodocid was even bigger than *Diplodocus carnegii*. Some early researchers thought they might be as much as 52m long but that may have been an exaggeration and we now think they were around 32m.

There's a mystery here. When the bones were found, scientists thought this dinosaur might be a massive 150 per cent bigger than *Diplodocus carnegii* and totally different in the way it looked. This dinosaur was originally called *Seismosaurus*, meaning 'earth-shaking lizard' but as the bones were cleaned, scientists realised that they didn't look that different and weren't that much bigger after all. So *Seismosaurus* vanished from the books and *Diplodocus hallorum* was introduced to the world in 1991.

DIPLODOCUS RELATIVES

Supersaurus vivianae (*super sore-us viv in-nay*)
'super lizard'

This sauropod lived about 153 million years ago. Fossils were first found in Colorado, USA, in 1972 and have since been found in Portugal.

30 m | 2 m

As with many of the diplodocids, there has been disagreement with the way *Supersaurus* is classified. To start with, it was put near *Barosaurus* and was very closely related to *Diplodocus*. Then the taxonomy changed and it was seen to be closer to *Apatosaurus*, not *Diplodocus*. And finally, it was back near *Barosaurus* again and is seen as one of the closest relatives of *Diplodocus*.

Galeamopus hayi (*gal-ay mope-us hay-i*) 'helmet head'

The skull of this dinosaur looked so thin and weak, scientists joked it would have needed a helmet.

Fossils date from around 155 million years ago and have been found in Wyoming and Colorado in the USA. Unlike many sauropods, we know what the skull looked like as one was found alongside an almost-complete skeleton.

Dinosaur Detectives

TEST YOUR DINO KNOWLEDGE HERE!

How long was the biggest *Diplodocus*?

What does the word sauropod mean?

What did *Diplodocus* eat?

When was the first *Diplodocus* discovered?

What was *Diplodocus hallorum* first named?

All the answers are in the text and at the back of the book.

CHAPTER 3

DINOSAUR DISCOVERIES

WHEN AND WHERE

WHEN AND WHERE

The times when the dinosaurs existed can be split into three main chunks (what we call 'periods') and these are the **Triassic period**, the **Jurassic period** and the **Cretaceous period**. *Diplodocus* was around towards the end of the Jurassic. At the end of the Triassic, there was a huge extinction, which the dinosaurs luckily survived (unlike the one at the end of the Cretaceous). This meant that at the start of the Jurassic, there was a lot of space for new species to evolve and within a few million years, there were loads of dinosaurs of all shapes and sizes.

There were some REALLY huge dinosaurs out there ... and *Diplodocus* was one of the longest ever to have lived. The biggest, *Diplodocus hallorum*, could be as much as 32m long. Stand in a park and ask the adult you're with to take 32 big steps away from you. THAT'S how big these dinosaurs were!

When and Where

One group that did do well was the Jurassic sauropods. There were many species, but *Diplodocus* appears to have been among the most common big dinosaurs at that time. The Jurassic lasted for 56.3 million years, from 201.3 million years ago to the beginning of the Cretaceous, 145 million years ago. *Diplodocus*, one of the best-known sauropods, lived during the late Jurassic, about 155.7 million to 150.8 million years ago.

During the early time of the dinosaurs, most of the land on Earth formed a huge supercontinent called Pangaea but during the Jurassic, this one big lump of land began to split into two major landmasses, Gondwana in the

THE WORLD IN THE LATE JURASSIC PERIOD

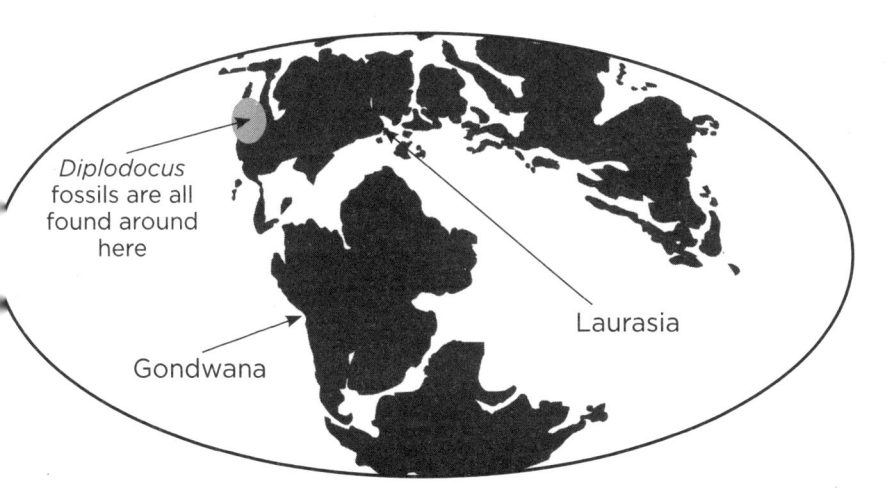

Diplodocus fossils are all found around here

Laurasia

Gondwana

Dinosaur Discoveries

Mesozoic Era

CRETACEOUS PERIOD

JURASSIC PERIOD

TRIASSIC PERIOD

← ***Diplodocus*** **were found from around the Late Jurassic**

46

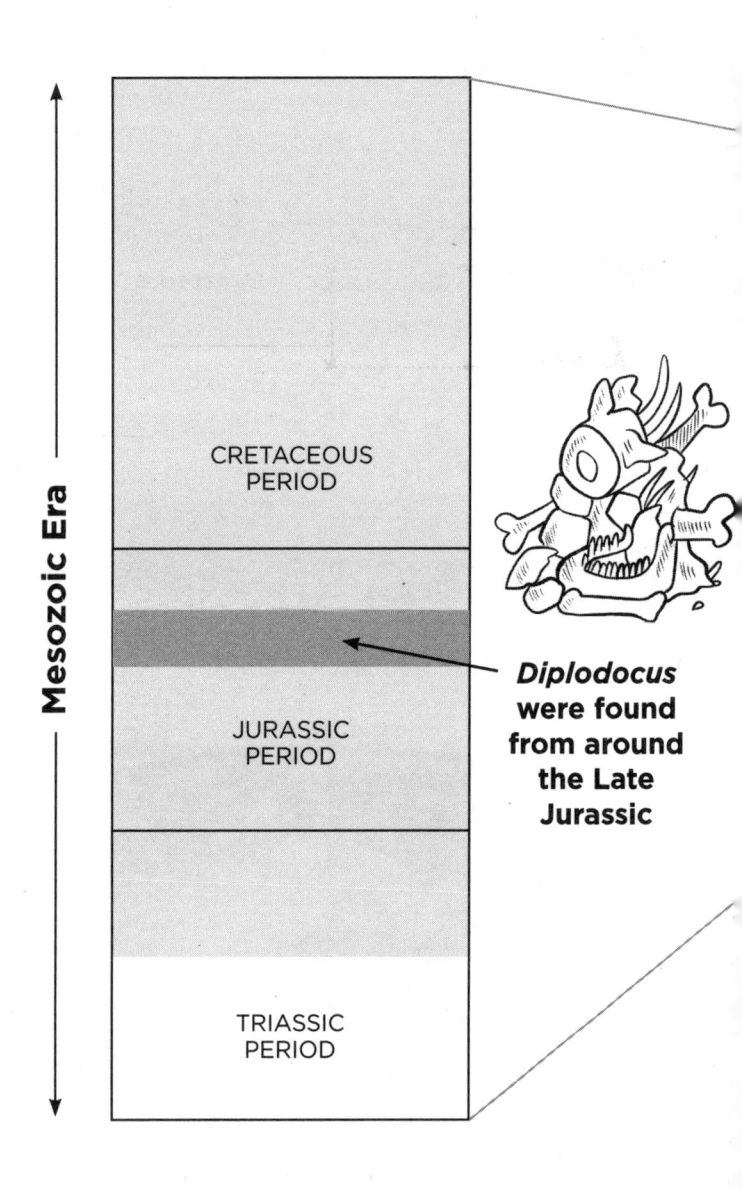

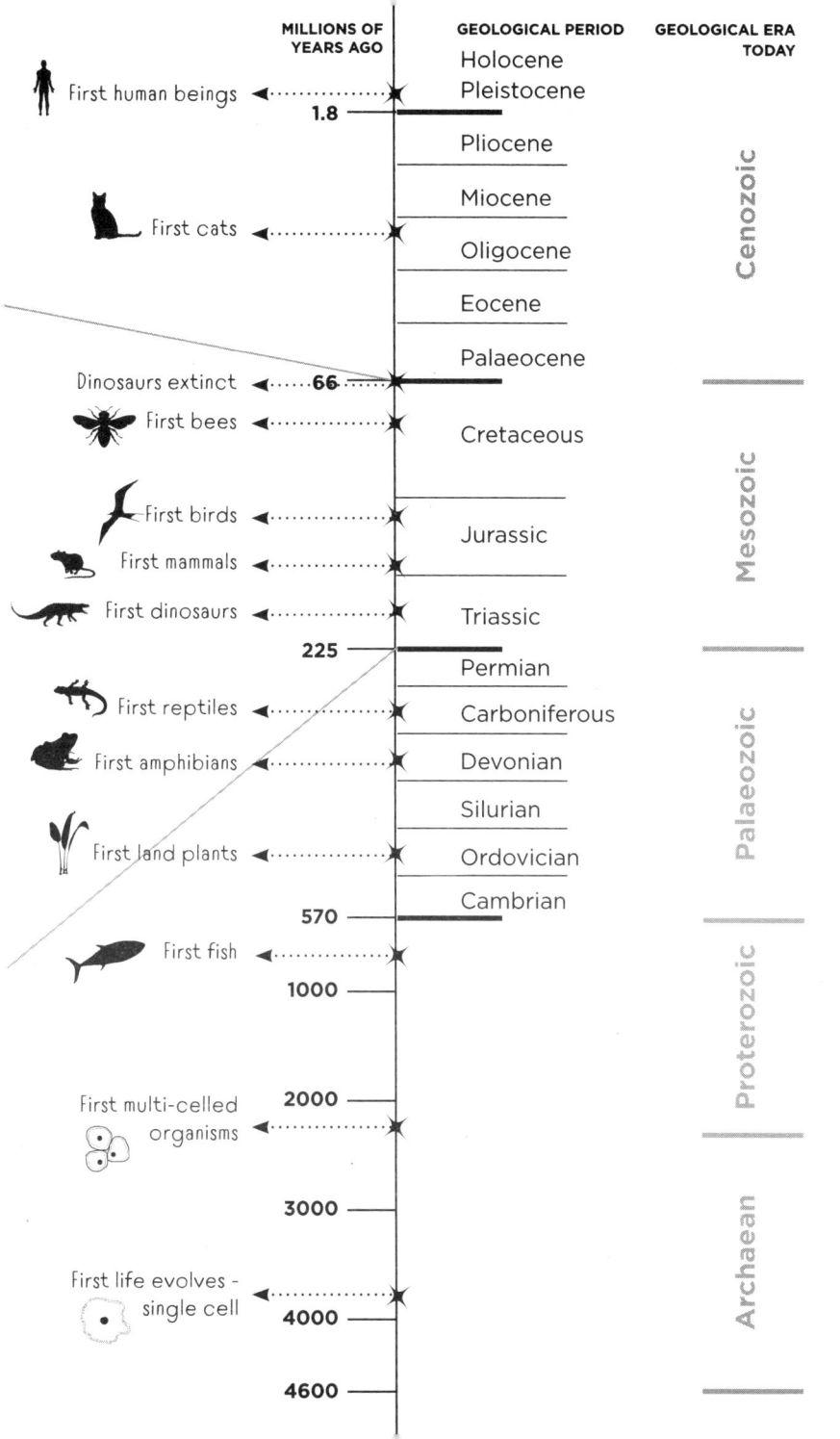

MILLIONS OF YEARS AGO	GEOLOGICAL PERIOD	GEOLOGICAL ERA TODAY
	Holocene	
1.8 — First human beings	Pleistocene	Cenozoic
	Pliocene	
	Miocene	
First cats	Oligocene	
	Eocene	
	Palaeocene	
66 — Dinosaurs extinct		
First bees	Cretaceous	Mesozoic
First birds	Jurassic	
First mammals		
First dinosaurs	Triassic	
225	Permian	
First reptiles	Carboniferous	Palaeozoic
First amphibians	Devonian	
	Silurian	
First land plants	Ordovician	
570	Cambrian	
First fish		Proterozoic
1000		
2000 — First multi-celled organisms		
3000		Archaean
4000 — First life evolves – single cell		
4600		

south and Laurasia to the north. *Diplodocus* fossils are now all found in certain places in the USA – the states of Colorado, Montana, Utah and Wyoming.

COULD A BRONTOSAURUS SIT ON YOUR LAP?

ASK AN EXPERT

So many people work with dinosaurs – from amateur collectors to world-famous scientists. Some go looking for fossils in the ground, others study them in laboratories and some recreate them as incredible pieces of artwork.

PROFESSOR KENNETH LACOVARA

Palaeontologist
Edelman Fossil Park of
Rowan University (USA)

Professor Kenneth Lacovara works at Edelman Fossil Park of Rowan University. He has unearthed some of the largest dinosaurs ever to walk the planet, including the super, massive *Dreadnoughtus*.

We asked Kenneth the following questions:

Could a *Brontosaurus* sit on your lap without killing you?

Could you stuff a *Brachiosaurus* in your backpack?

Could a *T. rex* fit in your sock drawer?

And this is what he told us:

'Yes, yes, and yes! Sounds crazy, but it's true, if we're talking about hatchling dinosaurs.

Baby dinosaurs were miniscule compared to their gigantic parents. When fully grown, the long-necked, long-tailed *Diplodocus carnegii* stretched the length of three double-decker London buses and weighed about 15 tonnes. Yet, this gargantuan beast hatched from an egg not much larger than an ostrich egg.

It's not clear whether *Diplodocus* mothers tended their nests, but either way, eggs in the wild are always in great danger. They make a tasty treat for any hungry predator. Worse still, *Diplodocus* embryos were slow to develop; one study estimates that they required more than 80 days. So dinosaurs, like *Diplodocus*, evolved strategies to spread the risk. They laid relatively small eggs, in clutches — not putting too many eggs in any one place. When the babies hatched, they were no larger than a cat.

We think that all dinosaurs were born small like this, though we haven't found eggs yet for every species. The fossilised embryos and hatchlings that have been found do not scale closely with adult body size. So, the 60-tonne behemoth *Dreadnoughtus*, which I discovered in South America, would have made a fine lap dinosaur when it hatched. Well, for a week or two. Dinosaurs grew fast, like whales do today. In very little time, it would have out-weighed you, on its way to achieving the mass of 13 African elephants!

Today, large mammals give birth to large babies, into which they pour loads of energy and care. Baby humans are relatively large, about 3.5kg on average, or about 1/22nd the weight of an adult. Baby elephants are born at about 90kg. Newborn giraffes are really big, about 102kg, or about 1/10th the weight of their parents. Killer whale babies are born at an impressive 160kg. But this pales in comparison to newborn blue whales. They slip into the world weighing the same as an adult hippopotamus, and grow to become the largest animals our planet has ever seen.

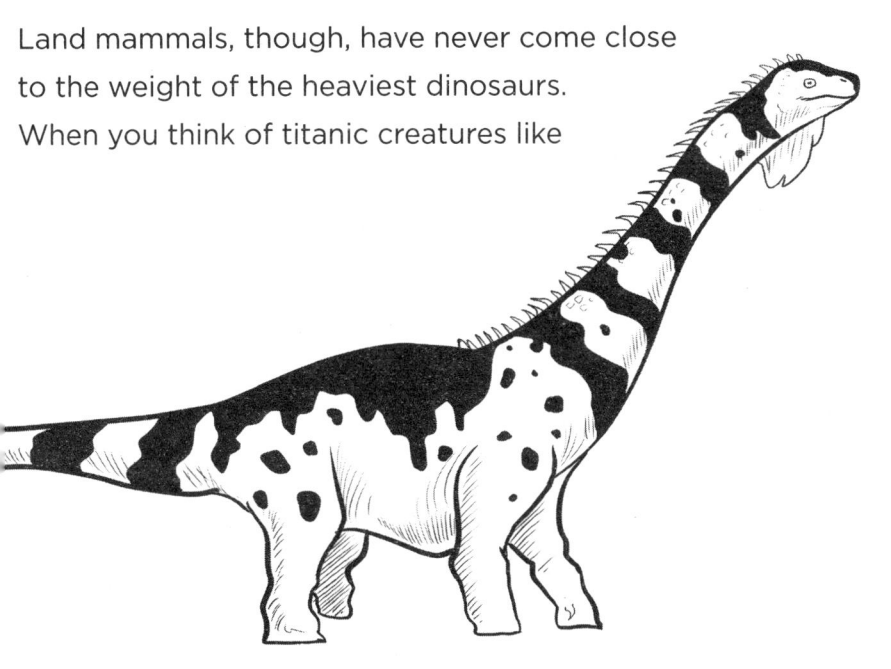

Land mammals, though, have never come close to the weight of the heaviest dinosaurs. When you think of titanic creatures like

Dreadnoughtus, go ahead and imagine them as huge. But remember, they were also tiny. And tiny dinosaurs did tiny dinosaur things. As hatchlings, they occupied the role of small plant-eating animals. As they grew, they did the job of sheep-sized herbivores, then cow-sized, elephant-sized, and so on up to animals the size of a herd of elephants. This must have been one of the keys to their success. As a single species, they could capture resources that today are divided among many species. In this way, dinosaurs that started off small and grew huge could extract as many calories as possible from the landscape, while making sure competition between members of their own species was as low as possible.

So, which weighs more, a *T. rex* or your dog?
The answer: It depends on the age of the *T. rex*.'

CHAPTER 4
DELVE INTO A DINOSAUR

ANATOMY OF A *DIPLODOCUS*

THE BONES

In some ways, sauropods like *Diplodocus* were like big elephants. In other ways, sauropods like *Diplodocus* were *nothing* like big elephants. Yes, they were big and yes, they were herbivores and okay, we think they lived in herds too, but sauropods had super-sized differences. Many had spines and bony armour and others had crazy crests on their heads, but the most obvious thing about them was that they were huge; making elephants look tiny by comparison. The anatomy of sauropods like *Diplodocus* had impressive adaptations, allowing them to become so big.

THE SKULL

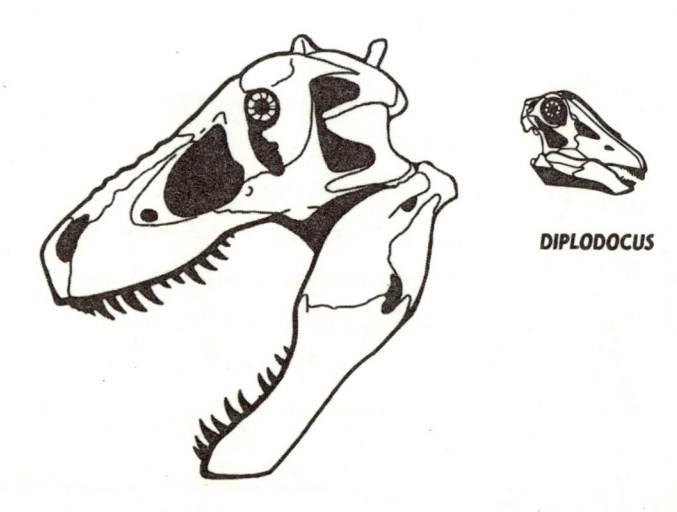

DIPLODOCUS

TYRANNOSAURUS REX

The Skull

Diplodocus may have been a prehistoric giant but it didn't need a big head. Compared to something like a *T. rex*, its head was tiny. It had a few teeth and they were all pretty small, made for stripping leaves, not heavy teeth for slashing or chewing food.

> Models of *Diplodocus* skulls have been used to see where biomechanical stress builds up. This sounds complicated but it's not. It's not the sort of stress you're thinking of – like worrying about homework or running out of your favourite cereal. It means where force builds up most in an object. When you are standing, the stress is spread across your foot but when you stand on tiptoes, all that stress goes into your toes. What you're feeling is the different biomechanical stress. In a *Diplodocus*, scientists tested different feeding behaviours to see where the stress was. When they tested bark stripping, there was way too much stress in the skull, but when they looked at leaf stripping from branches, the levels of stress were not high at all.

Delve into a Dinosaur

To understand why *Diplodocus* had a teeny head, we need to test your strength. Stretch your arm out straight and imagine it's a *Diplodocus* neck and whatever you hold in your hand is its head. First, hold out a melon or a large tin of baked beans.

Time how long you can hold it outstretched before your arm starts wobbling. Now do the same with an apple or a small tin of baked beans and see how long you manage this time. A lighter head at the end of the neck puts much less stress on the bones and muscles in the long sauropod neck.

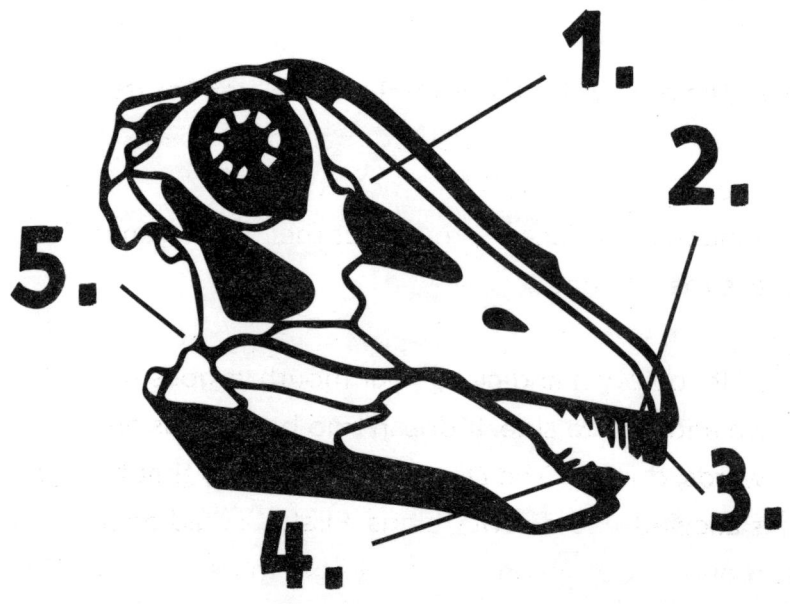

1.

2.

5.

3.

4.

The Skull

1. The part of the skull in front of the eye (the bone called the preorbital) was stretched out, making **the whole skull longer**. This meant that longer branches could be grabbed and more leaves stripped off with each mouthful.

2. Diplodocids have unusual teeth compared to other sauropods. They were long and slender and in cross-section, they were not circular or square but **elliptical, ending in a blunt, triangular point**.

3. Because their teeth were used for the same task and not chewing, the *Diplodocus* had homodont dentition – **all the teeth looked the same**.

4. *Diplodocus* had **teeth only at the front of its mouth**, allowing for specialised branch stripping. Diplodocids' teeth were like those of a shark, continuously replaced throughout their lives, generally in less than 35 days.

5. If you open and close your mouth, it goes up and down and side to side. It doesn't go backwards and forwards, does it? The *Diplodocus* could do that though. This allowed it to do two things. First, it could open its mouth wider, meaning it could get more food in.

Second, this allowed really fine adjustments to where its teeth sat and how they fitted together, so leaves could be stripped even more accurately.

When you eat your breakfast, different teeth do different things – sharp incisors at the front cut and 'snip' food into smaller pieces and cheek teeth (molars and pre-molars) do all the chewing. Easy! But **sauropods couldn't chew**. They had no big flat cheek teeth for chewing and in fact, they didn't have any cheeks. Instead, they had a row of teeth on the top and bottom jaw that looked like a row of fingers. Each one was long and thin and sauropods used them to strip leaves from trees, ferns and other plants.

Sauropod teeth differed between species, because they all fed in slightly different ways. They didn't all eat the same things or compete for food. **Diplodocids fed differently from any other dinosaurs** and we think they may have concentrated on softer leaves using one set of

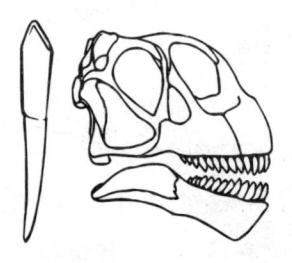

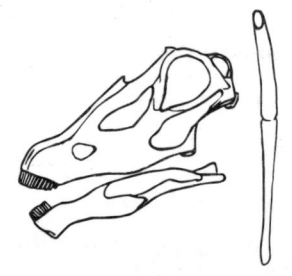

CAMARASAURUS   **DIPLODOCUS**

teeth at a time like a garden rake, pulling leaves off. The other set of teeth may have helped guide the first set and keep them stable.

THE SKELETON

A problem for early palaeontologists was how to imagine an animal that no human had ever seen. There were no photos or films of dinosaurs when they were alive, and sometimes scientists got things wrong. They thought that *Diplodocus* was so big and heavy that it must have lived in the water, sitting in rivers and lakes all day, keeping its head and tail afloat. Then scientists thought that maybe it held its head really high in the air and its tail dragged on the ground. We now know that *Diplodocus* walked in a more horizontal position, with its head and tail pretty much level and its legs acting like straight columns supporting its weight.

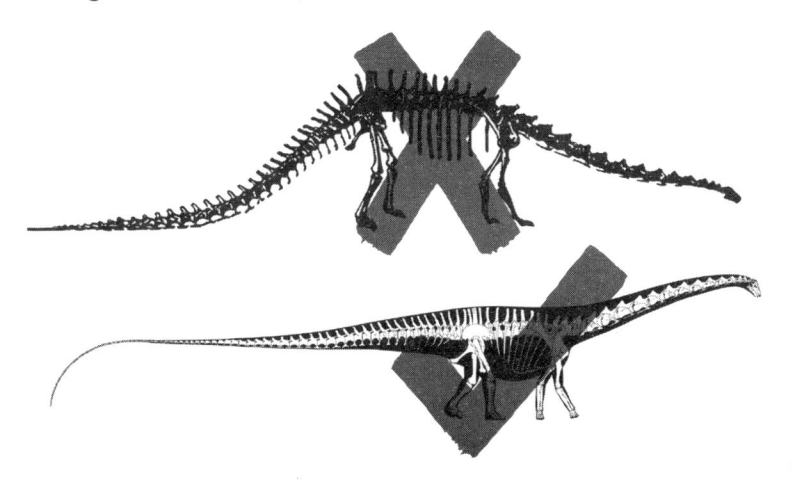

Delve into a Dinosaur

2.
Diplodocus vertebrae were incredibly fragile.

1.
Diplodocus had a huge tail, with over 80 vertebrae.

7.
The limbs had to be able to carry so much weight.

62

The Skeleton

3.

Long neck.
The *Diplodocus* had at least
15 vertebrae in the neck.

4.

Tiny head meant that
the neck wasn't under
huge levels of stress.

5.

The front foot (manus) of the
Diplodocus looked like those
seen in other sauropods.

6.

Diplodocus was a sauropod.
its hind feet had five toes
like a lizard.

Delve into a Dinosaur

1. ***Diplodocus* had a huge tail, with over 80 vertebrae, almost more than double the number found in some earlier sauropods.**

Even *Camarasaurus* (which lived at the same time) only had 53. But why was the tail so long? Well, there is some argument over this. Scientists agree that it would have acted as a balance for the rest of the body. It was also probably used against predators but here's the disagreement . . . was it used to whack big predators, such as *Allosaurus*, or was it used like a whip, making a terrifying cracking sound to scare off enemies? Scientists argue that if it was used as a whip, it would have caused huge injuries to the bones in the tail and although some injured bones have been found, there's still disagreement. What do you think?

2. ***Diplodocus* vertebrae were incredibly fragile.**

Even the very big bones in the neck were not solid; each was hollow and supported by a network of plates and struts. This made them very light when the animal was alive, so that the neck wasn't too heavy, but it also allowed for air sacs inside many of the bones. These air sacs helped these huge animals to breathe.

3.

Long neck.

Diplodocus had at least 15 vertebrae in the neck, whereas humans only have seven. To help keep the neck stable, special long pieces of bone, sat on the underside of the vertebrae. These are called 'cervical ribs' and overlap, to help muscles attach and to keep the neck strong.

The Skeleton

4. Tiny head.

It meant that the neck wasn't under huge levels of stress. We may never know but it's likely that *Diplodocus* was not a clever dinosaur, as its brain would have been tiny too.

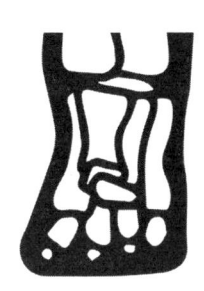

5. The front foot (manus) of the *Diplodocus* looked like those seen in other sauropods.

The five finger bones bunched together to form an upright column. It looks like a horseshoe in cross-section. *Diplodocus* front feet did not have claws apart from on one toe. But this claw was massive – and scientists still don't know what it was for.

6. *Diplodocus* was a sauropod, a name that means 'lizard foot', because its hind feet had five toes like a lizard.

Simple as that! But if you're a huge dinosaur and you weigh tonnes and tonnes, there's a real risk you'll be so heavy that you will injure yourself very easily. So the best thing was to walk on tiptoes. Yes, that's right – sauropods like *Diplodocus* walked on their toes. Elephants do the same. They both have big round fatty pads behind the toes in the back of their hind feet. These fatty pads act as shock absorbers and cushion a lot of weight. We walk on flat(ish) feet but the really big dinosaurs needed to tiptoe to avoid injury.

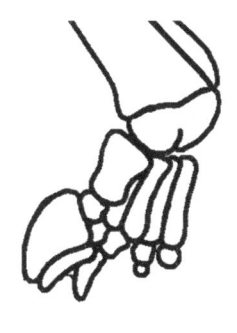

Delve into a Dinosaur

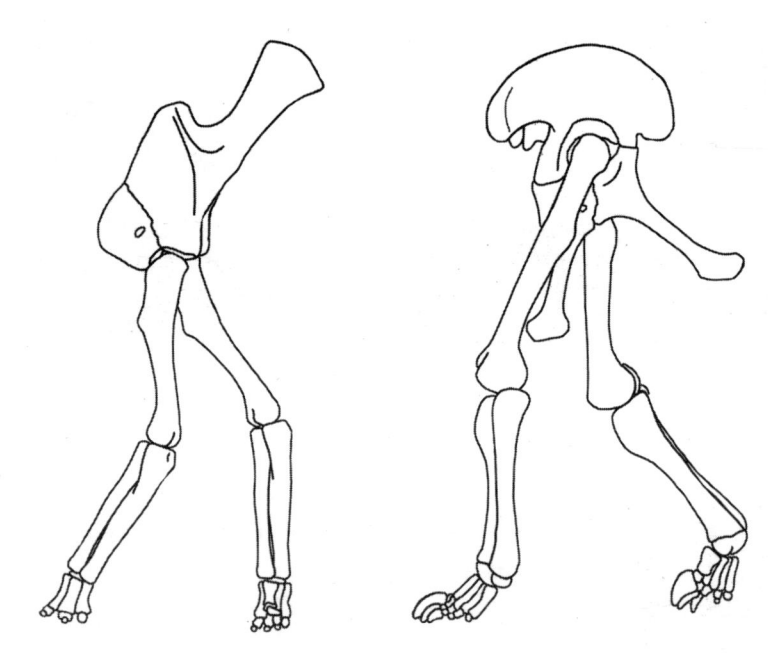

7. The limbs had to be able to carry so much weight.

Diplodocus (like any big sauropod) needed specially adapted legs to carry more than 15 tonnes (and much more in the titanosaurs). It managed to do this in a few ways. The first was to have legs like columns. Elephants are the same – their legs go straight up and the big round ball joint at the top of the femur joins the hip at the bottom of the pelvis, rather than at the side, as we see in other walking animals. The forearm bones had special adaptations too. They were able to lock together, so that they could carry the weight and not twist.

THE BODY

Some scientists think that some of the big sauropods needed to eat enough vegetation to fill a building skip each day. No time to chew! *Diplodocus* had eyes at the side of its head.

The Body

This may sound like a maths test but it's a fun Dino Quiz. If a really big *Diplodocus* weighed 15 tonnes and the average family car weighs 1.5 tonnes, what was the weight of a *Diplodocus* in cars?

There was very little overlap between what each eye could see, meaning it didn't have great 3D vision. It didn't need it, because it wasn't balancing in trees like monkeys, or chasing prey like wolves, both of which have forward-facing eyes. Like many prey species, *Diplodocus* needed to see as much as possible, spotting predators in its 'peripheral' vision.

Delve into a Dinosaur

THE BODY

2.

It is thought *Diplodocus* had pumping stations along the neck to enable blood to reach all parts of the body.

1.

The location of the nostrils on the *Diplodocus* has been much debated.

6.

The front legs were slightly shorter than the back legs.

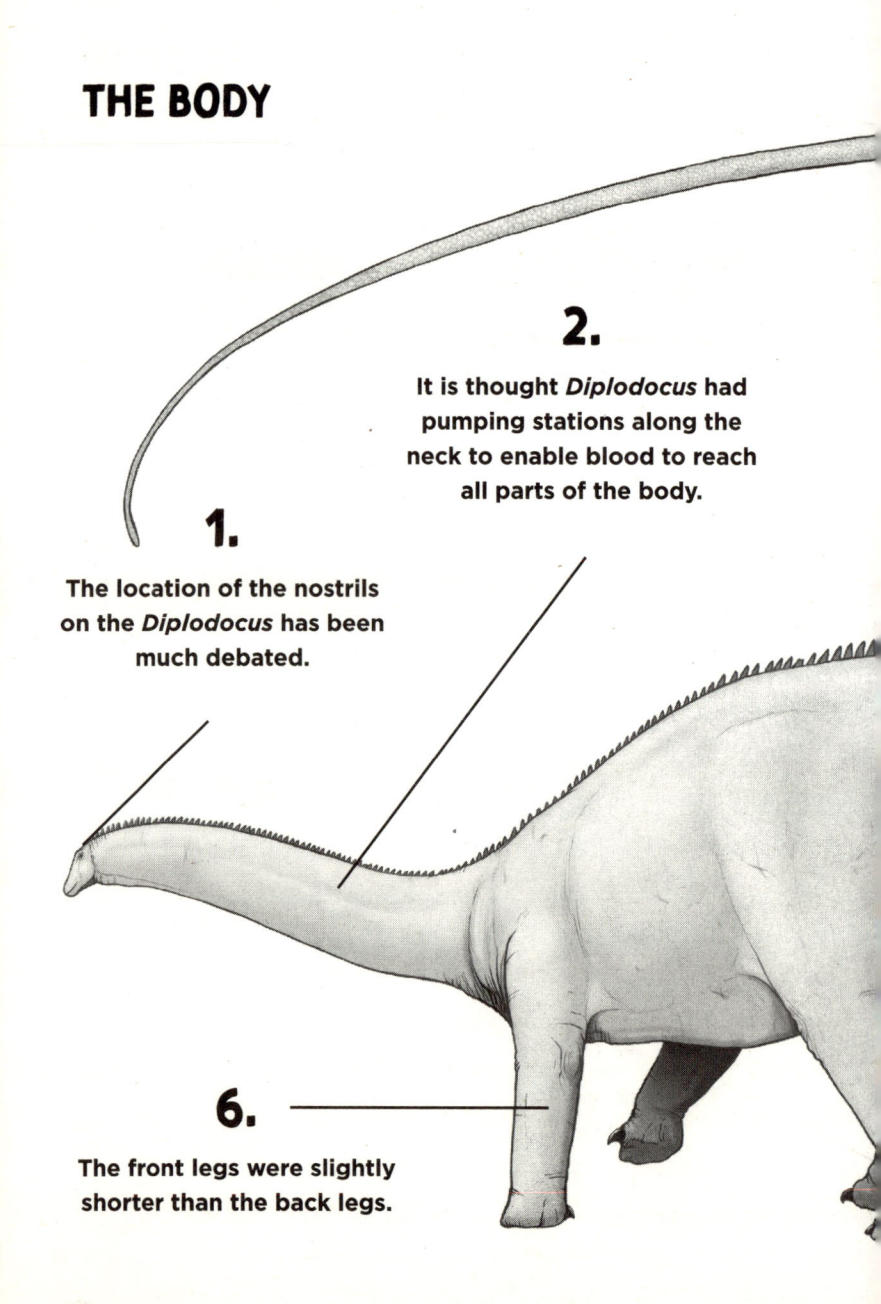

The Body

3.
Some are thought to have spines all the way from the head to the tip of the tail.

4.
It is thought that *Diplodocus* had the longest nerve cells that ever existed.

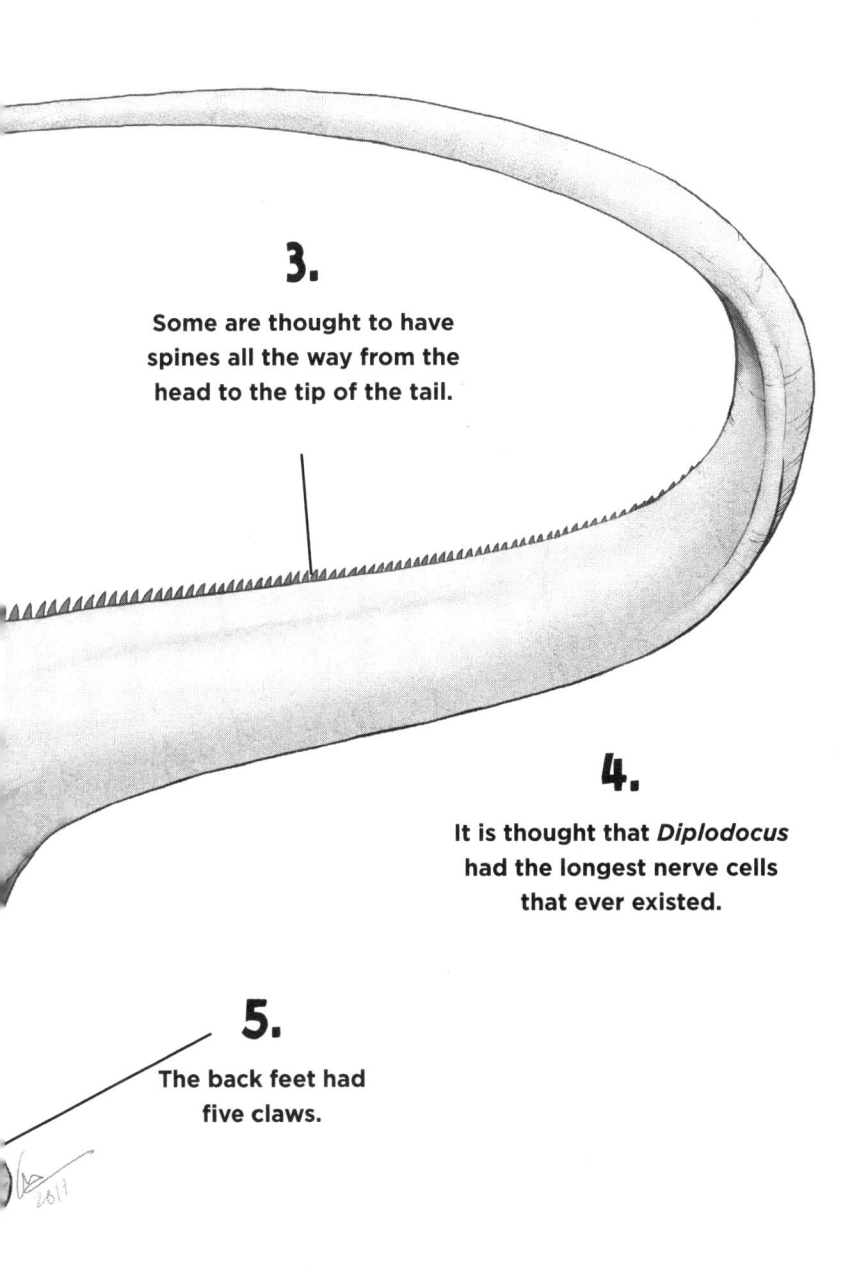

5.
The back feet had five claws.

Delve into a Dinosaur

1. Where are your **nostrils**? It's an easy question, right? Well, it's not so easy when asking where the nostrils on a *Diplodocus* were and it's been one of the weirdest and funniest arguments in palaeontology.

These are the different ideas scientists have had:

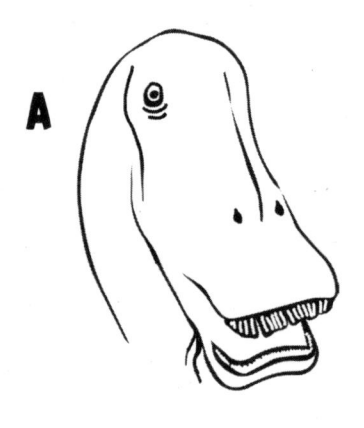

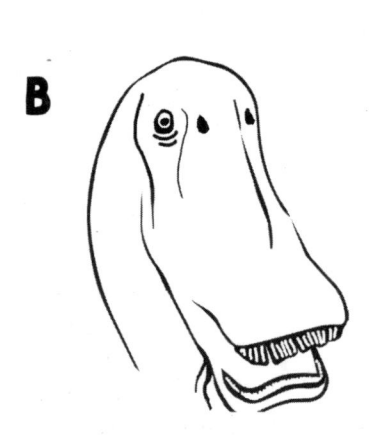

A) First, that the nasal openings in the skull were quite a long way back.
B) For a long time, scientists assumed that nostrils were on the top of the head, because they thought *Diplodocus* spent a lot of time in the water.
C) We now know it didn't need to spend most of its time in the water. Some scientists even thought *Diplodocus* had a trunk, like

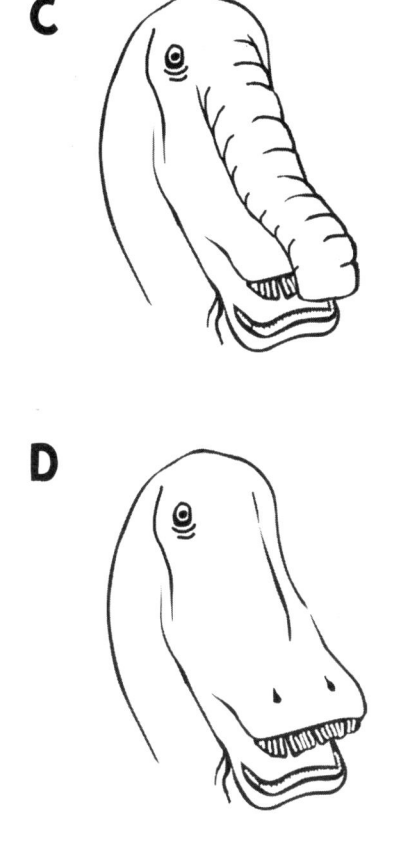

elephants. This might have helped it strip leaves from trees, but the shape of the skull means there was almost no chance it had a trunk.

D) We now think it had nostrils at the front of its head, at the top of the snout. Finally, the *Diplodocus* nostril mystery is solved.

2. Very approximately, your **heart** is about the size of your fist, perhaps a little bigger. We know how much blood we have, how often our hearts beat in a minute, day, year or even over a lifetime (if you're wondering, a hamster heart beats about 840 million times over its life and ours beats at least an incredible two billion times) but what about a sauropod's heart? Scientists have tried to figure out how big their hearts were and how they could pump blood around such big bodies. At first, some thought they must have had **hearts that weighed over two tonnes** (which would have been even bigger than a blue whale heart). But a heart this big would not have been possible, so scientists looked at other solutions and thought that maybe they had **extra pumping stations** along the **neck**. These would have acted like half-hearts, helping pump the blood to all parts of the body. But there's no evidence for this either and the truth is, we still don't know how *Diplodocus* and other sauropods pumped blood round their massive bodies. Yet.

3. We used to think that sauropods like *Diplodocus* had **smooth, scaly skin**, but some interesting fossil finds have helped us understand what it really looked like. A fossilised impression of some skin from a diplodocid showed that some species at least had tails with **long thin spines made of keratin** (the same stuff that makes up rhino horn, your hair and your finger nails). These spines may also have been on *Diplodocus* and may have been all the way from the **tip of the tail to the head**. These spines could have been **up to 18cm long**. It also had **armour under the skin**. Flat pieces of bone called **osteoderms**

The Body

protected sauropods like *Diplodocus* from predators and maybe from fights with other sauropods.

4. We think sauropods like *Diplodocus* had the **longest nerve cells** that ever existed and some would have extended from the back of the brain to the end of the tail right to the tip. If you stub your toe, you 'feel' it within milliseconds but if you pulled a *Diplodocus* by the tail (which would have been a mean thing to do) then it might have taken **one to two seconds** for its **brain** to register it.

5. The back feet had **five claws** but also had to be able to take a lot of weight. Some scientists think the claws **all stuck out individually** (like a tortoise) others think the claws sort of fitted together and acted like **one big blade**. This could have stopped *Diplodocus* slipping as well as absorbing some of its weight.

6. The **front legs** were slightly shorter than the back legs. This meant *Diplodocus* stood and walked in a **horizontal** position.

Delve into a Dinosaur

We don't really know how *Diplodocus* nerves worked. Was the body packed with nerve endings and sensitive to touch or were they spaced out, so that it could respond more quickly? Like us, it probably had some areas of the body that were more sensitive than others. Get someone to take two chopsticks and hold them 1cm apart. Close your eyes and ask them to gently poke the chopsticks against your fingertip. Can you feel them both? Now ask them to do the same on your back. How many chopsticks do you feel? If you feel a difference, then that's because the nerve endings in your fingertips are packed closer together than they are on your back. Try it again with the chopsticks further apart – at what point can you feel them both on your back?

CHAPTER 5
DINOSAUR DOMAINS

HABITATS AND ECOSYSTEMS

Dinosaur Domains

HABITATS AND ECOSYSTEMS

The time when *Diplodocus* walked the Earth (155.7 – 150.8 million years ago) is known as the Late Jurassic and this was a time when we see an explosion of dinosaur species. In fact, the parts of North America where *Diplodocus* fossils are found (Colorado, Montana, Utah and Wyoming), as well as other areas such as New Mexico, Oklahoma, South Dakota and Texas are known for having more dinosaur fossils than anywhere else in the world. As well as *Diplodocus*, there was a whole range of dinosaur characters around at the same time. *Allosaurus*, for example, which was the top predator in that part of the world, account for more than 70 per cent of the theropod fossils found. They were everywhere!

Dinosaur Domains

The Middle Jurassic was very hot and dry but this all changed and the Late Jurassic was humid and wet and would have looked and felt a bit more tropical. With this change in climate came a big change in the plants too. Cycads (which looked like palm trees but were very different), conifers such as pine trees, ginkgo trees, tree ferns and Araucaria (or 'monkey puzzle') trees would all have been part of a sauropod's diet.

It's difficult to be 100 per cent certain about what *Diplodocus* ate, but looking at its teeth gives us an idea. There's a lot of disagreement between scientists about how the sauropods held their necks . . . could they stretch up high above their body or were they held out more horizontally? We still don't know and until we do, we don't know whether *Diplodocus* could get leaves from the very tall monkey puzzle trees or could only pluck leaves from plants closer to the ground. We do know that *Diplodocus* could stand on its back legs though, so maybe it could reach the highest leaves after all.

Fossils are often found in bands of sediment. Sometimes these are very small bands and sometimes they're pretty big, spanning millions of years. *Diplodocus* fossils are found in what we call the

Morrison Formation. It's in North America and dates from 154–152 million years ago. *Diplodocus* fossils are one of the most commonly found species in this area from this time but the Morrison Formation seems to have been the time of the sauropods, because lots of other species of huge herbivores have been found there, meaning they all lived at around the same time. These species include:

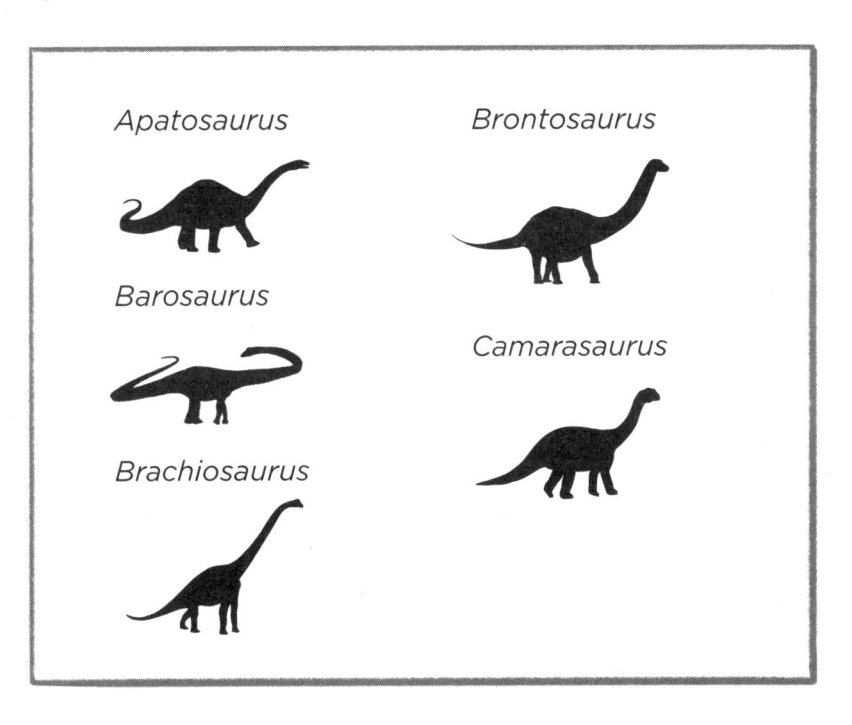

Apatosaurus

Brontosaurus

Barosaurus

Camarasaurus

Brachiosaurus

But there obviously weren't just sauropods at the end of the Jurassic – there was a mix of well-known and less-common dinosaurs:

Dinosaur Domains

Allosaurus

Amargasaurus

Camptosaurus

Ceratosaurus

Dryosaurus

Gargoyleosaurus

Koparion

Ornitholestes

Habitats and Ecosystems

Othnielia

Stegosaurus

Stokesosaurus

Torvosaurus

If you are lucky enough to go out and find a *Diplodocus* skeleton, then keep your eyes peeled for other species often found at the exact same locations:

Apatosaurus

Allosaurus

Camarasaurus

Stegosaurus

Dinosaur Domains

TEST YOUR DINO KNOWLEDGE HERE!

When did *Diplodocus* live?

How many vertebrae did *Diplodocus* have in its tail?

Name one of the relatives of *Diplodocus*.

How much did *Diplodocus* weigh?

What was the weather like in the Late Jurassic?

All the answers are in the text and at the back of the book.

NEW GIANT DINOSAUR DISCOVERIES

NEW SCIENCE

The dinosaurs, apart from the birds, all died out about 66 million years ago, right? But the weird thing is that the dinosaur family is still getting bigger and bigger. It's not just little dinosaurs that are being discovered. Recently, a whole bunch of new giant sauropods have been discovered, adding to the more famous *Diplodocus* and *Brachiosaurus* and the huge *Argentinosaurus* and *Dreadnoughtus*.

Although they're massive and make up roughly a quarter of all the dinosaur species we know so far (not including those modern dinosaurs, the birds), there are lots of things we still don't know about the sauropods.

Even though sauropod skeletons are big, their fossil bones are fragile and can easily break. Our bones are dense and full of thick spongy marrow. But the bones from dinosaurs such as sauropods were different – more like the bones of birds. Many people call them hollow but they're not . . . they're air-filled (or pneumatised – 'noo-ma tie-zd') and yes, there is a difference. It's all about the struts, remember.

During the fossilisation process, these fragile bones often broke, fell apart and became twisted over thousands and millions of years. The bones in the long neck were fragile, so are frequently missing when sauropods are found. Even some of the stronger bones are crushed after 100 million years or so underground, with hundreds of tonnes of earth and rock pressing down on them.

Because sauropod skeletons are often in pieces with bits missing, every new fossil find can reveal so much more about these giant dinosaurs. Imagine what it was like for palaeontologists when four new sauropods from four entirely different (and new) groups were found very recently (just before this book was written, in fact). The four new dinosaurs are *Tengrisaurus starkovi*, *Vouivria damparisensis*, *Moabosaurus utahensis* and *Galeamopus pabsti* and they're all very, very cool.

Sometimes, a new discovery can come from an old find and *Vouivria* is a good example of this. These bones were found in 1934, but very recently scientists realised that they were from a brand new group of sauropods. *Vouivria* appears to be an early member of the group that included *Brachiosaurus*. This group of sauropods were successful and have been found in Africa, North America and South America, so hopefully *Vouivria* can help tell us why the group did so well.

Sometimes, you only need a little bit of a skeleton to know you are dealing with something new and this is the case with sauropods. Because bones such as its tail vertebrae are so weird and different, only a few pieces confirmed that *Tengrisaurus starkovi* was a new dinosaur – not just a sauropod, but a titanosaur, one of the super-big sauropods. Towards the start of the Cretaceous, many of the sauropods had become extinct but the titanosaurs were thriving and this period was full of these super-sized sauropods. The newly discovered *Tengrisaurus* was one of the first titanosaurs to evolve, so although not much of it has been found, it tells us a lot about how the titanosaurs evolved.

An amazing number of bones – around 5,500 – from another sauropod from the same time as *Tengrisaurus*, were found. These were from lots of different individual dinosaurs but no complete skeletons were found. With so many bones, scientists were able to piece together exactly what *Moabosaurus* looked like. Although the huge number of bones means that work has only just started on this early titanosaur, *Moabosaurus* helps us further understand what life was like for giant herbivores during the Early Cretaceous period.

This is a skeleton. It's made up from different skeletons from different individuals (because the scientists haven't found a full one yet). Making a skeleton like this is called a 'composite skeleton'.

The group *Galeamopus* was first named in 2015, making it a pretty new group anyway but since the first species was discovered, another has been found – *Galeamopus pabsti*. These two newly discovered dinosaurs were closely related to *Diplodocus* and lived during the Late Jurassic. Unlike *Diplodocus*, scientists have found some brilliant fossil skulls for *Galeamopus*. This sounds great but this new dinosaur has thrown up a few mysteries. One of the main skeletons looks like a mixture of young and old animals, so this means there's even more about dinosaurs we still don't know.

Discoveries are always important – they reveal not only new species of sauropods but also new groups of sauropods, from different parts of the world and from different times in history. Remember, studying dinosaurs is a bit like a jigsaw. Every dinosaur discovery is another piece in the puzzle and helps us understand that little bit more each time. Just imagine how many more giant dinosaurs are yet to be discovered.

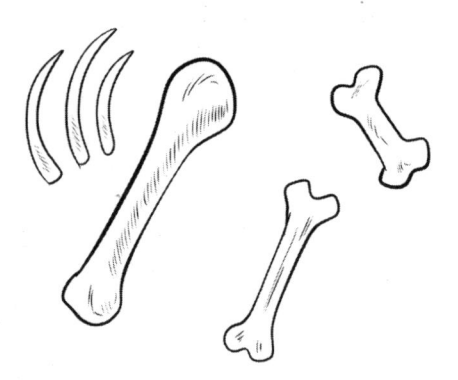

CHAPTER 6
DODGING DINOSAURS

EVOLUTIONARY ARMS RACE

EVOLUTIONARY ARMS RACE

There are lots of things that drive evolution, making a species change over time. It could be a particular habitat, such as the hot desert and camels, or feeding techniques (just think about giant anteaters and their long snouts and very long tongues) but it might be down to a competition between predators and prey. The term for this is an evolutionary arms

> Sometimes an evolutionary arms race is all about which species is the most sneaky. On the coral reefs in the Indian Ocean, two species are locked in a very weird evolutionary arms race. The bluestreak cleaner wrasse is a little fish about as long as an adult human finger and is blue and yellow, with a long black streak along its body. This brightly coloured little fish even does a special dance and is allowed to go near big fish on the reef, like the groupers, to pluck parasites off their skin and even clean their teeth.

race. Whereas the predator species evolves in a way to increase its chances of catching and eating prey, the prey species (because it doesn't want to end up as lunch) evolves to reduce the chances of ending up as a meal. Then, in turn, the predator evolves to increase its chances and so on and so on. It never ends and both species are trying to do what is best for them.

> But another little reef fish looks the same, apart from one thing – it has a massive pair of canine teeth that extend up into the upper part of its skull.
>
> After the small changes made through the evolutionary arms race, the sabre-toothed blenny looks like the cleaner wrasse and even dances like it but it wants to take a bite out of the big fish. It has evolved to look just like the cleaner wrasse, because the big fish all trust them.

THE BATTLE

It is during a ferocious Jurassic storm one evening that we see a *Diplodocus* about to battle for her life. Up above a beach, past the high tide line, is a clearing where a wide shallow river flows beside a vast forest. There's a herd of *Diplodocus* feeding here. Over 20 of the huge sauropods stand together, swaying their long necks through the vegetation, pulling branches through their mouths to strip off the soft leaves.

This group is led by a mature adult female and with her sisters and aunts, she protects five young calves, only a couple of years old but already as tall as elephants and each as long as a bus. The females stand in a circle around their young, protecting them from any would-be predators. As the storm hits the shoreline, our herd of herbivores huddle together, standing with their heads away from the wind and stinging rain. Sounds are drowned out and it's hard to see through the downpour. But just at the edge of the forest, nestled among giant green ferns, is a huge *Allosaurus*. It has watched the group for two days, waiting for an opportunity.

The Battle

Waiting for the chance to kill.

Sometimes, the *Allosaurus* hunts in
a small pack, but after a vicious fight
broke out while scavenging a stegosaur kill,
this one has left his group and is hunting alone. His
large, forward-facing eyes follow the swaying heads of
the sheltering *Diplodocus* herd. Weighing about eight
times less than a fully grown *Diplodocus*, the *Allosaurus*
knows he must wait until he can hunt a smaller, weaker
youngster. But then he spies one of the herd all alone.

In the shallow riverbed, an old female *Diplodocus* rests
against the riverbank, sheltering from the worst of the
wind. She's separated from the rest of the herd and they
cannot see her. But the *Allosaurus* can. He stretches his
legs and stalks towards her. He keeps his body low as he
runs, head down and ready to ambush her.

The *Allosaurus* leaps off the riverbank and strikes the
Diplodocus, dragging his sharp-clawed toes down her
huge, grey back. His claws cut deep but not for long,
because the flat pieces of bony armour beneath her skin
stop them from doing too much damage.

The old *Diplodocus* twists sharply and throws the *Allosaurus* off. He moves to her side, ready to bite her vast, soft stomach. He knows that if the rest of the herd notice, they will rush over to protect her. He needs to kill quickly.

The *Allosaurus* is much faster and moves around easily as the old female stomps at the ground with her huge feet, warning him off. She turns further so her tail faces the would-be predator and swipes it dangerously through the air. They both know that one hit from that long, muscular tail would be deadly. She lashes it again and again, so hard that the bones in her own tail tip actually fracture.

The *Allosaurus* moves fast, away from the tail. He bites into her thigh, using his large head like an axe, slamming down into her muscle. Dozens of sharp, serrated teeth dig into the flesh and the old *Diplodocus* bellows in pain.

The *Allosaurus* moves off, leaving several teeth embedded in the old animal. Now the *Diplodocus* is injured, the *Allosaurus* hopes to make a quick kill and moves towards her head. Although an *Allosaurus* would never usually risk attacking a fully grown sauropod, he might just be in luck this time.

As the giant predator targets the vulnerable neck of the *Diplodocus*, he looks up and sees the rest of the *Diplodocus* herd. Alerted by the call of the injured old female, they have rushed over to help. In that moment, the *Allosaurus* loses his concentration and turns away from the old female.

The 15-tonne sauropod rears on to her hind legs, towering high above the *Allosaurus*. Resting on her damaged tail, she lunges and falls onto her attacker. Her huge feet crash down on the back of the *Allosaurus*, killing him instantly.

The old female *Diplodocus* kicks his broken body aside and snorts loudly and angrily. She sways her huge tail aggressively, in pain but still alive.

Dodging Dinosaurs

The Battle

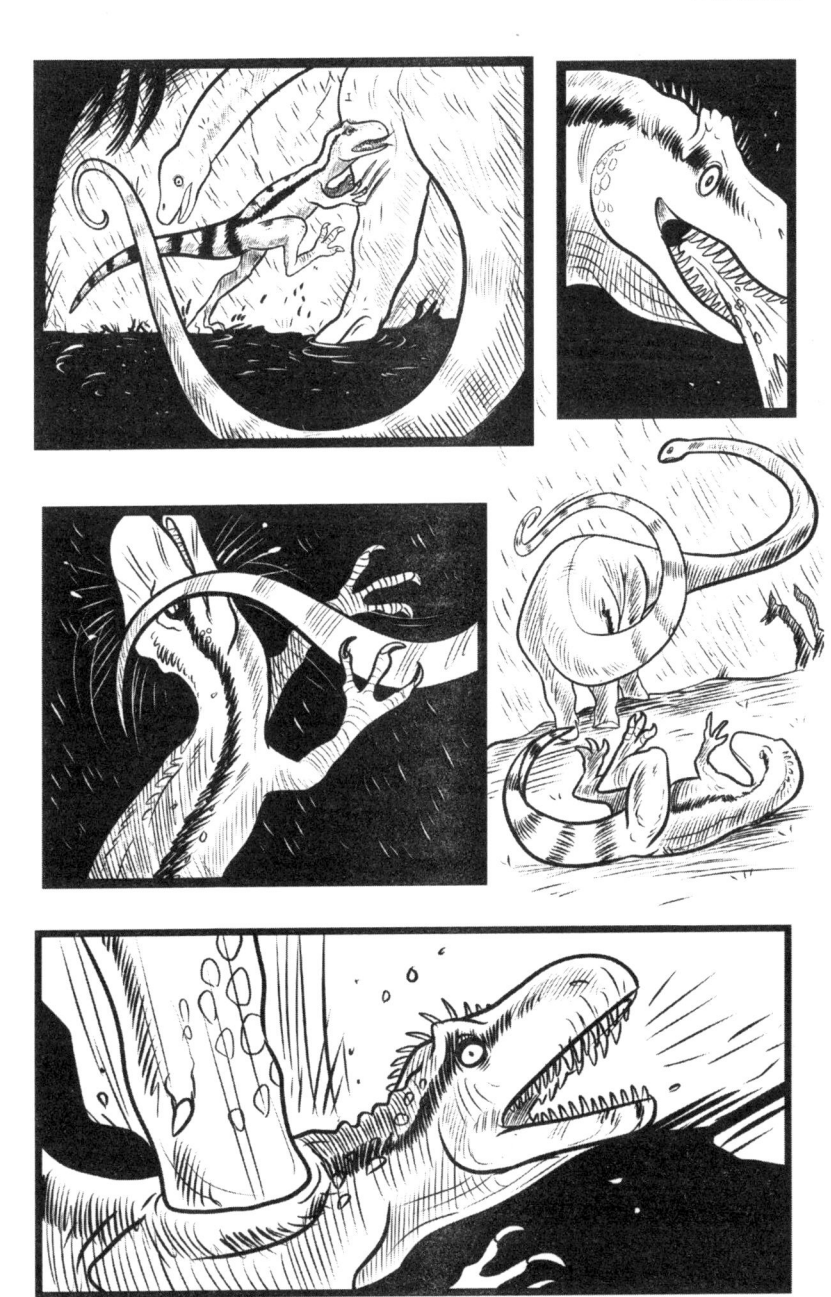

Dodging Dinosaurs

She joins the rest of the herd and slowly, they move away as the storm continues, leaving the deadly *Allosaurus* in the mud, the victim of a terrible mistake.

ALLOSAURUS

SPEED	8
AVERAGE WEIGHT (tonnes)	4
AGILITY	7
WEAPONS (teeth, horns)	8

DIPLODOCUS

SPEED	2
AVERAGE WEIGHT (tonnes)	9
AGILITY	2
WEAPONS (teeth, horns)	5

FOSSIL FINDER

PRACTICAL

We all want to go out and find an amazing fossilised skeleton from a brand new species of dinosaur. But first, it helps to understand what makes a fossil, so that you can know where to look and how to make sure you preserve any fossils you find. How are fossils formed? There are a few different ways fossils can be made but here is one of the most common methods of fossilisation.

1. After an animal dies, it sinks to the seabed and is buried by sediment.

As a marine animal dies, it sinks and rests on the sea floor. All the soft parts decompose and rot, leaving the skeleton. The bones quickly become completely buried by sand and mud. This makes the marine environment the perfect place to create fossils, explaining why marine fossils are so common.

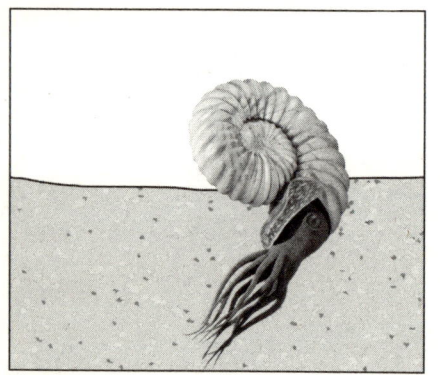

2. Over time, sediment around the bones begins to harden.

Over tens of thousands of years, more and more sediment builds up above the bones. As the seabed is added to more and more, the pressure around the bones increases. The sediment begins to harden and turn to rock.

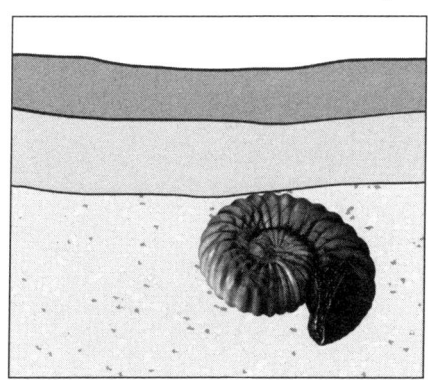

3. The bones dissolve, forming a fossil 'mould'.

With the sediment around the bones now hard, dissolved minerals within the ground dissolve the bones themselves. This leaves a 'hollow' in the sediment. This 'mould' is a perfect imprint of the original bone.

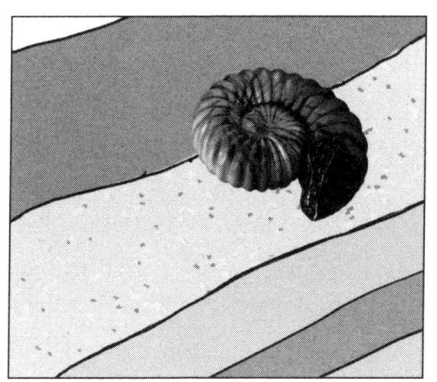

4. Minerals collect inside the mould, making a cast.

Ground water is full of minerals, which seeps into the mould, filling the cavity. These minerals are left behind in the mould and a perfect cast is formed. This cast has the same shape as the original bones, but has none of its internal features.

Other fossils form when the mineral-rich groundwater dissolves the bones and replaces it there and then with the minerals. In these fossils, the internal structures of the bones are also all preserved.

5. The fossil is exposed.

After millions of years underground, seas retreated and what was once beneath the sea is suddenly on dry land. The sediment is eroded by wind and rain. Eventually, layers of earth are removed and the fossil ends up near the surface, ready for you to find it.

Although this is a common way for fossils to be formed, they did not all start under the sea. Many animals fossilised on land and were covered by sand or soft sediment from rivers or lakes.

So, now we know what a fossil is, but if there were so many animals and plants alive during prehistoric times, why don't we find hundreds of fossils every time we take a walk through the park or visit the beach?

Well, conditions have to be just right. The decay of an animal needs to be under certain conditions to help increase the chances of fossilisation, such as low levels of oxygen – for example, when an animal sinks into muddy sediment at the bottom of the sea – or a fast burial, when an animal is buried by a sand storm.

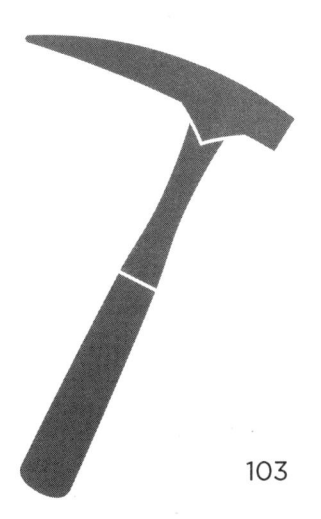

QUIZ ANSWERS

P 42

How long was the biggest *Diplodocus*?
As much as 32m.

What does the word sauropod mean?
Lizard foot.

What did *Diplodocus* eat?
Plants.

When was the first *Diplodocus* discovered?
1877.

What was *Diplodocus hallorum* first named?
Seismosaurus.

P 67

How many cars would weigh the same as one Diplodocus?
Ten cars.

P 82

When did *Diplodocus* live?
Towards the end of the Jurassic period.

How many vertebrae did *Diplodocus* have in its tail?
About 80.

Name one of the relatives of *Diplodocus*.
Supersaurus vivianae or *Galeamopus hayi*.

How much did *Diplodocus* weigh?
About 15 tonnes.

What was the weather like in the Late Jurassic?
Humid and wet.

How many did you get?

GLOSSARY

Araucaria This is the scientific name for monkey puzzle trees. They are very tall trees with long branches made up from triangular, spiky leaves.

Diapsid Means 'two arches'. These animals have two holes in the back of the skull, tucked away just behind the eye. Diapsids include all lizards, snakes, tortoises, turtles, crocodiles, dinosaurs and birds (even though they are dinosaurs too). Some diapsids have lost one of these holes (lizards), or both holes (turtles, tortoise and snakes). Some diapsids, such as birds, look very different but still count because that's how they would have started.

Diplodocidae The group that included *Diplodocus*, *Barosaurus* and *Galeamopus*. These sauropods were thinner than some others and they were very long. Their legs were fairly short but the back legs were longer than the front legs.

Diplodocid This name can be used to talk about any of the species in the group Diplodicidae.

Epipophyses These look like bony little wings in the neck vertebrae, found in dinosaurs.

Fibula This bone sits next to the tibia and connects to it at the top and bottom end. It is the thinnest of the three 'big' bones in the hind leg.

Ornithischia Sounds like '*orn-iss-thick ee-ar*' and means 'bird-hipped', because the pelvic bones of these dinosaurs looked similar to those of birds, even though they're not really related. This was a very broad group and included things like the horned dinosaurs, such as *Triceratops*, armoured dinosaurs such as *Stegosaurus* and duckbilled dinosaurs, like hadrosaurs. Most of this group were herbivores.

Saurischia Sounds like '*sore-iss chee-ar*' and means 'lizard-hipped', because their pelvic bones looked similar to those seen in lizards. These dinosaurs included theropods, sauropods and birds.

Sauropod These dinosaurs had very long tails and very long necks. They had small heads (for the size of their body) and they had four big, straight legs. Some grew to huge sizes and were the biggest animals ever to walk on land.

Synapsid Means 'fused arch'. These animals have a single hole in the back of the skull, tucked away just behind the eye. Humans and all other mammals are synapsids. So were some earlier groups of animals that are now extinct but which were related to mammals.

Titanosaur A group within the sauropods. These were the super-sized sauropods, such as *Dreadnoughtus* and *Argentinosaurus* and were most commonly found during the Cretaceous.

Theropod These were two-legged dinosaurs. Although they first evolved as carnivores, later on there were carnivorous, omnivorous and even herbivorous theropods. Today, birds are the only surviving theropod dinosaurs.

Trochanter Any of the bony lumps found along the top part of the femur (thigh bone). Muscles attach to these trochanters.

PICTURE CREDITS

Adobestock: 1, 2, 3, 30, 36–37, 41, 66, 67, 79, 80, 81, 92, 93, 94, 98, 100, 101, 103.

Depositphotos: 1, 2, 3, 16, 17, 18, 25, 26–27, 28, 34, 35, 66, 67, 79, 81, 83.

Ethan Kocak: 5, 6, 9, 11, 15, 19, 22, 23, 29, 42, 43, 44, 46, 49, 50, 52–53, 54, 55, 57, 58, 67, 74, 75, 82, 83, 86, 87, 88, 89, 90, 96, 97, 99, 105, 107, 113.

Gabriel Ugueto: 68–69.

Scott Hartman: 20–21, 38, 39, 48, 56, 58 (skull), 61, 62–63, 64–65, 66.

NOTE from **SCOTT HARTMAN**:

Diplodocus: This is based on the excellent Carnegie Museum specimen (CM 84). It was dug up in what is now Dinosaur National Monument in Utah, and is probably the most famous skeleton in the world, as it is the basis for all of the casts of *Diplodocus* that were sent out to international museums in the early 20th century. It's complete except for the tail, which I've filled in from other specimens.

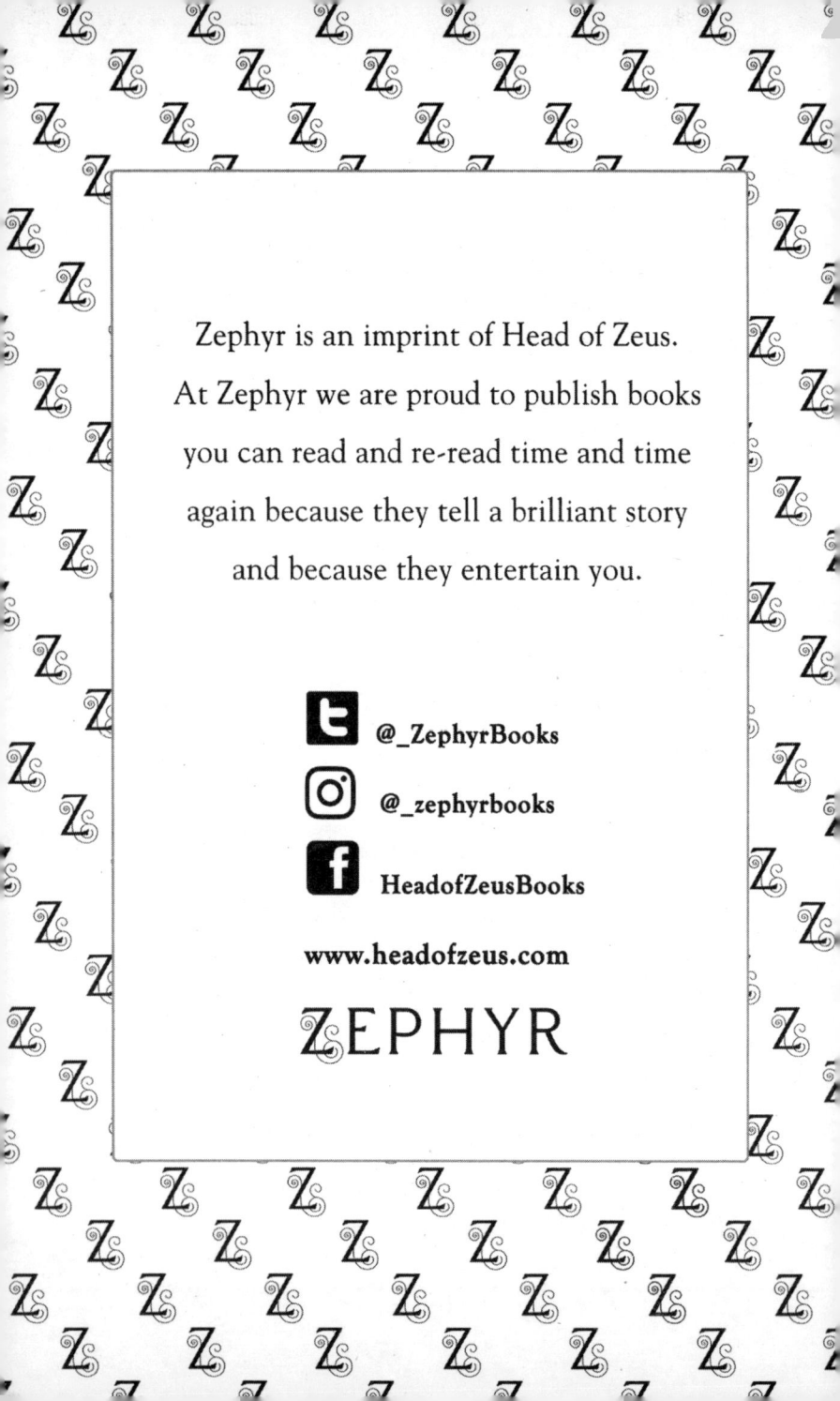

Zephyr is an imprint of Head of Zeus. At Zephyr we are proud to publish books you can read and re-read time and time again because they tell a brilliant story and because they entertain you.

@_ZephyrBooks

@_zephyrbooks

HeadofZeusBooks

www.headofzeus.com

ZEPHYR